D1566117

THE DISFIGURED FACE

THE DISFIGURED FACE

Traditional Natural Law and
Its Encounter with Modernity

LUIS CORTEST

Fordham University Press NEW YORK 2008

Library of Congress Cataloging-in-Publication Data

Cortest, Luis.
The disfigured face : traditional natural law and its encounter with modernity /
Luis Cortest.
p. cm.
Includes bibliographical references (p.   ) and index.
ISBN-13: 978-0-8232-2853-9 (cloth : alk paper)
1. Thomas, Aquinas, Saint, 1225–1274.   2. Natural law.   I. Title.
B765.T54C645   2008
171'.2—dc22   2008003069

Printed in the United States of America
10 09 08   5 4 3 2 1
First edition

In loving memory of Tomás Daniel Cortest
(January 30, 1991–May 15, 2006)

Contents

Introduction

On May 5, 1888, Pope Leo XIII issued one of his lesser-known encyclicals, *In Plurimis*.[1] This document, written in part to express the Roman pontiff's personal joy on hearing of the legal abolition of slavery in Brazil, includes a memorable description of how slavery as a human institution had long been defended in principle and in practice by non-Christians:

> Even those who were wisest in the pagan world, illustrious philosophers and learned jurisconsults, outraging the common feeling of mankind, succeeded in persuading themselves and others that slavery was simply a necessary condition of nature. Nor did they hesitate to assert that the slave class was very inferior to the freemen both in intelligence and perfection of bodily development, and therefore that slaves, as things wanting in reason and sense, ought in all things to be the instruments of the will, however rash and unworthy, of their masters. Such inhuman and wicked doctrines are to be specially detested; for, when once they are accepted, there is no form of oppression so wicked but that it will defend itself beneath some color of legality and justice.[2]

The doctrine condemned in this passage is clearly that which we now call "natural servitude," that is, the teaching that some men are born slaves or are slaves by nature. Indeed, this was the very doctrine defended by Aristotle in the first book of his *Politics*. In the encyclical, Pope Leo briefly traces the long history within the Christian tradition of attempts to combat this inimical doctrine. It would seem most appropriate that Leo would invoke this tradition at precisely the moment when slavery as a legal institution would finally be eradicated in the New World. The legal and philosophical battle concerning this issue began centuries before the encyclical was written. This most bitter war of words would lead eventually to the transformation of many modern American and European legal and social institutions.

It is clear that Leo was very suspicious of certain legal traditions. The pope's words here are quite strong: "there is no form of oppression so wicked but that it will defend itself beneath some color of legality and justice." The Roman pontiff understood that different legal and philosophical arguments can be used by clever advocates to defend any form of oppression and wickedness. Leo himself often speaks of law, but the legal tradition he invokes is that of natural law. For Leo, natural law provides the only solid foundation for a legitimate doctrine of human rights in which the dignity of the human person can be fully protected.

In a general sense, the notion of natural law is probably as old as Western European culture. Anyone who has read Sophocles' great tragedy *Antigone* can see that this doctrine was already present in classical Greek thought. We also find natural law frequently described in Roman legal texts. One of the most important of these descriptions is found in Cicero's *De legibus*. In book 1 of this text Cicero informs us that every man has a sense of law implanted in him by nature:

> But in fact we can perceive the difference between good laws and bad by referring them to no other standard than Nature; indeed, it is not merely Justice and Injustice which are distinguished by Nature, but also and without exception things which are honourable and dishonourable. For since an intelligence common to us all makes things known to us and formulates them in our minds, honourable actions are ascribed by us to virtue, and dishonourable actions to vice; and only a madman would conclude that these judgments are matters of opinion, and not fixed by Nature.[3]

It is important to note that for Cicero, it is not merely an innate notion of law that all of us possess, but also a sense of justice and a notion of what constitutes virtue and vice. Cicero also informs us that these matters are "fixed by Nature."

In the Middle Ages there are many authors who write on this subject, but none has been more influential than Thomas Aquinas. For centuries after Thomas's death, his discussion of natural law served as the model for countless theologians and jurists. The clearest statement of his view is found in *Summa Theologiae*, I, II, question 94, article 2: "The precepts of the natural law are to the practical reason what the first principles of demonstrations are to the speculative reason; because both are self-evident."[4] For Thomas, natural law constitutes the first principles of practical reason. Thomas treats this subject in several of his works. One of the best illustrations of this notion can be found in the commentary on book 5 of Aristotle's *Nicomachean Ethics*:

> In speculative matters there are some things naturally known, like indemonstrable principles, and truths closely connected with them; there are other things discovered by human ingenuity, and conclusions flowing from these. Likewise in practical matters there are some principles naturally known as it were, indemonstrable principles and truths related to them, as evil must be avoided, no one is to be unjustly injured, theft must not be committed and so on; others are devised by human diligence which are here called just legal enactments.[5]

This relationship between natural law and legal precepts is fundamental for any application of natural law principles to a given legal system. For Thomas, natural law must be understood within the context of natural justice. An excellent explanation of this doctrine is found in the same Aristotelian commentary, where "natural justice" is distinguished from "legal" justice:

> But since natural justice exists always and everywhere, as has been pointed out, this is not applicable to legal or positive justice. On this account it is necessary that whatever follows from natural justice as a conclusion will be natural justice. Thus, from the fact that no one should be unjustly injured it follows that theft must not be committed—this belongs to natural justice. In the other way something can originate from natural justice after the manner of a determination, and thus all positive or legal justice

arises from natural justice. For example, that a thief be punished is natural justice but that he be punished by such and such a penalty is legal justice.[6]

For Thomas, the reason that one can speak of a "natural justice" or moral principles that are known naturally is because nature and morality conform to an immutable ontological order. That is to say, nature itself is a reflection of the order of "being." This point is absolutely critical for our understanding of Thomas's moral philosophy. Thomas makes this point very clearly in book 3 of his *Summa contra gentiles*:

> There must be definite kinds of operations which are appropriate to a definite nature, whenever things have such a definite nature. In fact, the operation appropriate to a given being is a consequent of that nature. Now, it is obvious that there is a determinate kind of nature for man. Therefore, there must be some operations that are in themselves appropriate for man. Moreover, whenever a certain thing is natural to any being, that without which this certain thing cannot be possessed must also be natural, "for nature is not defective in regard to necessary things." But it is natural for man to be a social animal, and this is shown by the fact that one man alone does not suffice for all the things necessary to human life. So, the things without which human society cannot be maintained are naturally appropriate to man. Examples of such things are: to preserve for each man what is his own and to refrain from injuries. Therefore, these are some things among human acts that are naturally right.[7]

Without this ontological dimension the Thomistic system is incomplete. One can construct a moral philosophy on the basis of a set of rules of practical order, but without the ontological foundation, the system cannot accurately be called "Thomistic" in the original sense.

The development of natural law, however, does not continue along a single line. By the middle of the seventeenth century, natural law begins to take on a new meaning. For John Locke, natural law becomes the discernment of moral principles based on the observation of nature. This notion of natural law, which I will call the "modern" version, begins with the observation of nature and then proceeds to a discovery of general moral principles. Perhaps the clearest statement on the question can be found in Locke's *Essays on the Law of Nature*:

> This law of nature can be described as being the decree of the divine will discernible by the light of nature and indicating what is and what is not in conformity with rational nature, and for this very reason commanding or prohibiting. It appears to me less correctly termed by some people the dictate of reason, since reason does not so much establish and pronounce this law of nature as search for it and discover it as a law enacted by a superior power and implanted in our hearts.[8]

It should be noted that this work was composed by Locke early in his career. Leo Strauss offers 1664 as the likely date of composition.[9] Strauss has also observed that these essays show quite clearly that Locke, already at this stage in his career, found it difficult to accept the traditional notion of natural law.[10] One of the reasons that Locke and his followers would have found the modern understanding of natural law more acceptable is that their conception of nature was quite different from that of writers (both pagan and Christian) from previous times. These earlier authors, for the most part, embraced a teleological idea of nature. This view, established by Aristotle, was the primary model for understanding nature well into the seventeenth century. Locke and philosophers of later generations approach nature more empirically. Thus, this modern doctrine of natural law is understood like the laws of motion: in both cases one discovers how things work on the basis of observation.

More fundamental than the contrasting views of nature are the profound philosophical differences that distinguish these two traditions. The modern notion of natural law rejects not only Aristotelian teleology but also ontology. For Aquinas, moral principles are conceived as an extension of the first principles of "being." His moral doctrine can not be separated from his ontology. This feature is precisely what differentiates his system from those of most modern thinkers. A good example of this point would be the moral philosophy of Immanuel Kant. Moral science for Kant is non-ontological; it is constructed on the basis of universal imperatives, which are themselves not connected to any notion of being. Ultimately, in the Kantian system, we acknowledge the universal application of moral principles because they conform to reason. We do not have to believe that at a deeper level reason itself and moral principles are valid because they conform to an ontological reality. It is in fact the case that much of what we now call "deontological" morality has as its point of departure the thinking of Kant.[11]

The modern notion of positive rights (that is to say, rights that grant us the power to do something rather than merely to be protected from some harm) developed along with modern natural law. John Locke, Thomas Jefferson, and the early nineteenth-century "liberals" embraced this new understanding of rights rather than the old doctrine. Some scholars have observed that already in the Middle Ages we find writers who defend "natural" or "human" rights.[12] It should be noted, however, that these early "rights" tend to be of the negative sort (the rights that protect us rather than empower us) except in the case of property. The reason for this is that medieval writers were (with a few notable exceptions) more concerned with the notion of justice than with personal rights. When the doctrine of *jus* (right) is described, it is talked about in terms of the right ordering of things. We see this clearly in the works of Thomas Aquinas.[13] Some recent scholars such as John Finnis have argued that Thomas was also a proponent of positive rights.[14] In this book I show that Aquinas did not anachronistically defend this modern doctrine. What we do find in Thomas's works is not a doctrine of "rights," but rather a strong notion of justice and a defense of the dignity of the human person, created in God's image.

One of the most important moments in the development of natural-law doctrine occurred in sixteenth-century Spain. At that time a group of Spanish Dominicans from Salamanca (now called the "School of Salamanca") participated in a series of juridical and philosophical debates concerning the legitimacy of the Spanish Conquest of the New World. The most influential of these writers, Francisco de Vitoria, was also the leading Spanish Thomist of his day. In his works we find carefully constructed arguments concerning just-war theory and the "rights" of human societies. Vitoria and his followers (Melchor Cano,

Domingo de Soto, and Domingo Báñez among them) were theologians interested in morality, justice, and law; the guiding principles of their arguments are found in the works of Thomas Aquinas. Hugo Grotius later read the texts of these Spanish authors, and they served him as important sources in the development of modern international law. It should be noted, however, that while Grotius did adopt many of the ideas of jurists from the School of Salamanca, he did not accept their Thomistic (ontological) foundation. Grotius knew the works of the Thomists very well, but he may well not have had the same command of the texts of Thomas himself.

The phenomenon of knowing the ideas of the disciples rather than those of the master is not uncommon in the history of philosophy.[15] In the case of Aquinas, this is quite often true. The Spanish Jesuit Francisco Suárez (1548–1617), who taught at the universities of Alcalá, Avila, Coimbra, Salamanca, Segovia, and Valladolid and the Roman College, was without question the most influential philosopher in the Thomistic tradition (his thought will be discussed at length in chapters 1 and 3).[16] After Suárez's death, his *Disputationes Metaphysicae* became the standard text for the study of Thomistic philosophy for the next two hundred years.[17] In later centuries, many philosophers would come to know Thomas's thought exclusively through the works of Suárez. In the nineteenth century, when Pope Leo XIII and others challenged the principles of liberalism and other modern ideas, they appealed to the teaching of Thomas Aquinas, but, in fact, many of the most important Thomists of that time were Suarezians.[18] The Thomistic tradition was still alive, but Thomas's works were studied far less than those of his commentators. Pope Leo, however, was more interested in the thought of Thomas himself than in the works of his commentators.[19] Only after the appearance of the papal encyclical *Aeterni Patris* in 1879 was an effort made to prepare a reliable edition of the works of Thomas Aquinas. Pope Leo initiated this project because he firmly believed that Thomas's philosophy could provide the principles for a Catholic defense against the challenges of the new ideas that had been shaped by modern philosophy.

Leo could see that traditional natural law doctrine was beginning to disappear. He understood clearly that the new understanding of nature brought about by the experimental and social sciences in the nineteenth century was destroying the old order. He also knew that these new ideas were based on modern philosophical principles. Leo's predecessor, Pius IX, had condemned quite a number of "current errors" in the *Syllabus of Errors* in 1864.[20] Leo, however, was not content merely to attack or condemn these ideas; he wanted to mount a legitimate philosophical challenge. For that very reason, he initiated the revival of Thomism with *Aeterni Patris*.[21]

Cardinal Désiré Mercier, a Belgian Thomist greatly influenced by Pope Leo, used Thomistic natural-law principles to condemn German war crimes committed against his countrymen during World War I. Mercier, a brilliant scholar and teacher, understood the moral implications of traditional natural law as few others have since that time. His eloquent philosophical defense of his country stands in sharp contrast to the pronouncements of so many modern jurists, whose arguments are informed by neither philosophy nor any sense of natural law. After Mercier there are few defenders of traditional natural law. One of those who does defend this doctrine is the French philosopher Jacques Maritain, who tried to reconcile natural-law doctrine with the modern notion of human rights. His thought has had a great impact on Catholic intellectuals for several decades. Curiously, the one place where traditional natural law has survived is in the Roman Catholic Church. In the twentieth century, several popes defended the doctrine. Perhaps the strongest defender of this tradition was John Paul II, a great admirer of Leo XIII. In his 1991 encyclical *Centessimus Annus*, commemorating the hundredth anniversary of *Rerum Novarum*, the Roman pontiff produced a commentary on Pope Leo's text and addressed the social and moral problems of the late twentieth century, using the same Thomistic principles as those used in *Rerum Novarum*. John Paul's 1993 encyclical *Veritatis Splendor* may be described accurately as one of the most important natural-law texts produced in the twentieth century. *Fides et Ratio*, issued in 1998, provides a clarification of the guiding philosophical principles for Catholic philosophers and theologians; here again we see the importance of Thomistic thought and in particular, the ontological foundation of morality so fundamental for traditional natural law.

This book has a threefold purpose: to describe the character of traditional natural law as it was developed by Thomas Aquinas and later reformulated by sixteenth-century Spanish Neothomists; to show how this doctrine has fared in its encounter with modern secular philosophy from the seventeenth century to the present; and to show how natural law in its traditional, Thomistic form has survived almost exclusively in several key encyclicals of the Roman Catholic Church, where the principles of the older doctrine have been used to challenge the overpowering influence of modern secular culture.

THE DISFIGURED FACE

Chapter One

THOMISTIC ONTOLOGY

Before we can begin to examine Thomistic moral philosophy and its relationship to modern ethical systems, it is imperative that we understand the distinguishing feature of Thomas's moral thought, its ontological foundation. Ontology, in simple terms, is the science of being. Thomas considered "being" the first and most fundamental object known by reason. Thomas's ontology was based, to a large extent, on an Aristotelian model. Although Aristotle did not call his science "ontology," his metaphysics takes us to the heart of the matter.

Aristotle described metaphysics as "a science which investigates being as being and the attributes which belong to this in virtue of its own nature." The Stagirite then explained how metaphysics differs from all other fields of inquiry: "None of these others deals generally with being as being. They cut off a part of being and investigate the attributes of this part—this is what the mathematical sciences for instance do."[1] Clearly, for Aristotle, metaphysics could never be reduced to a philosophy of science. Although Aristotle's notion of metaphysics or First Philosophy is quite complex, at least one of its primary meanings corresponds to that branch of philosophy we moderns call ontology.

The science that Aristotle considered the highest has been under constant assault virtually since the eighteenth century. In fact, for many thinkers, metaphysics or ontology is no longer considered an object of serious philosophical investigation:

> Above all it is *metaphysics*, as structure and object of thought, that is continually being proclaimed dead. The critical effort of Kant's discussion of metaphysics was still directed at the idea of

its possibility, but, at least since Auguste Comte, it has been banished from philosophy as a fruitless mental exertion, the delusive "enchanter" of thought and speech, characterized by rigid dogma, productive only of false problems and obscuring the real question. The invectives, particularly those of the present, spring from a variety of motives and aims: Adorno, for example, together with the so called "Critical School," sees metaphysics or first philosophy (including transcendental philosophy in this category) as a *system of identity*, both enslaving and itself slave to the mental concept, which is summarily dismissed as a close neighbor of totalitarianism and so the chief culprit for a social order which is itself a closed system, an ensnaring web lethal to everything that does not subscribe to identity. . . . Neopositivism and linguistic philosophy are responsible for the charge that all metaphysics is meaningless: it presents problems which actually are only illusory ones, that is to say, they talk about something which cannot be talked about; they are nothing but an illusion similar to that of poetry, a spell cast by the *language* of metaphysics, the remedy for which lies in "a restoration of words from their metaphysical to their everyday usage." This is the conclusion to be drawn from the thesis that one can make a statement only about something "which is the case," i.e. something which is empirically verifiable. Other statements, which concern the non-empirical and aim at the construction of a "system," must consequently be labeled as "mystical," in a pejorative sense.[2]

Ironically, the Middle Ages, a period many moderns consider of lesser importance in the history of philosophy, was an age of great innovation in ontology. The developments in the science of being that take place in the thirteenth century remind us of the history of theoretical physics in the late nineteenth and early twentieth centuries. In both cases, a revolution of sorts takes place.

Indeed, if atomic theory was redefined by physicists such as Albert Einstein, Ernest Rutherford, Wolfgang Pauli, Werner Heisenberg, and Niels Bohr on the basis of a new principle of mechanics and a theory of relativity, metaphysics also was restructured by philosophers such as

Albert the Great, Thomas Aquinas, William of Auvergne, Henry of Ghent, and John Duns Scotus. Aquinas was clearly the greatest philosopher of his time, and it is in his thought that we find the most significant development in ontology. From this group of thinkers, Thomas Aquinas, the Angelic Doctor, is the philosopher who most stressed the importance of existence in our understanding of being. Joseph Owens, in his now-classic study *The Doctrine of Being in the Aristotelian Metaphysics*, observes that the whole question of existence is absent from that book:

> The essence of a thing may be fully known without any knowledge of whether the thing exists or not. The notion of a "mountain of gold" can be fully understood without knowing whether such a thing has ever actually existed. Or—to take an example in the category of Entity—the essence of an Aristotelian separate Entity might be treated without knowing whether it *exists* or not. But the Stagirite never raises such a question. The problem in this form is simply not present in the *Metaphysics*.[3]

For Aquinas, existence is the most fundamental principle of all reality:

> The most perfect thing of all is to exist, for everything else is potential compared to existence. Nothing achieves actuality except it exist, and the act of existing is therefore the ultimate actuality of everything, and even of every form. So it is that things acquire existence, and not existence things. For in the very phrases "the existence of man" or "of a horse" or "of some other thing," it is existence that is regarded as an acquisition like a form, not the thing to which existence belongs.[4]

This conclusion, which might seem insignificant to those who are concerned primarily with the philosophy of language, is of profound importance for our apprehension of reality. To understand the full significance of this principle, perhaps a couple of points should be considered.

On one hand, if the notion of existence is excluded from ontological speculation, we begin to lose contact with the physical world; our observations become purely conceptual or formal. On the other hand, if we are not concerned primarily with existence, the truth of propositions is lost in endless speculation about the possible and that which is not self-contradictory. Concerning the Thomistic notion of existence and its role in ontological judgments, Etienne Gilson has said:

> Because things are, true judgments are true inasmuch as they accept them as actual beings, and, because to be a "being" is primarily to be, *veritas fundatur in esse rei magis quam in ipsa quidditate*: truth is more principally grounded in the existence (*esse*) of the thing than it is in its essence. . . . Both reality and our knowledge of it entail the subjective actualization by existence of an essential objectivity. Being *qua* being is their very unity. Unless such knowledge of reality be possible, no knowledge will ever grasp reality such as it is.[5]

In the years immediately following Aquinas's death in 1274, his reputation seems to have suffered somewhat. The reasons for this surprising development are difficult to discern. Bishop Tempier's condemnation of 219 propositions at Paris in 1277 may have contributed to the decline of the great philosopher's reputation; however, only about sixteen of these propositions could actually be said to apply to Thomas.[6] Nonetheless, for a period of about forty years the Angelic Doctor had only a few defenders.[7] By the late 1320s, William of Ockham had become an influential (although very controversial) figure in theological circles. Although he never realized it, Ockham, or the "Venerable Inceptor" as he was sometimes called, would later be called the father of "nominalism," the philosophical doctrine that would dominate European thinking for more than 150 years.[8]

The strength of nominalism would seem to be its rigorous logical structure. In ontological analysis, this logical rigor results in a principle of reduction. A number of the most fundamental principles of Thomistic metaphysics are rejected by nominalism. As an example of this change in perspective, we might consider Ockham's discussion of the relationship between essence and existence:

> Since we have touched upon "existence" (*esse existere*), we shall make a digression for a while and consider how the existence of a

thing is related to the thing, i.e. whether the existence of a thing and its essence are two entities extra-mentally distinct from each other. It appears to me that they are not two such entities, nor does "existence" signify anything different from the thing itself. For if there were something distinct, then it would be either a substance or an accident. But it is not an accident, because in that case the existence of a man would be a quality or quantity, which is manifestly false. . . . Nor can it be a substance, because every substance is either matter or form, or a composition of matter and form, or a separated substance. But it is manifest that none of these can be called the existence of a thing, if existence is a thing distinct from the essence (*entitas*) of the thing itself. Furthermore, if essence and existence were two things, then either they would constitute something that is intrinsically one, or they would not. If they did, then the one must be actuality and the other potentiality; hence the one would be matter and the other form; but that is absurd. . . . We have to say, therefore, that essence (*entitas*) and existence (*existentia*) are not two things. On the contrary, the words "thing" and "to be" (*esse*) signify one and the same thing, but the one in the manner of a noun and the other in the manner of a verb.[9]

Clearly, William of Ockham rejects the fundamental Thomistic distinction between essence and existence. His critique bears a striking resemblance to the arguments made by modern philosophers of language. By limiting the application of terms, Ockham limits the range of the argument, thus transforming Aquinas's fundamental philosophical distinction into an absurd, self-contradictory proposition. Already in the early fourteenth century the decline of Thomistic ontology was evident. For those who imagine that this decline is not important, it should be noted that the followers of Ockham inspired a completely different kind of thinking than that defended by Thomas. Thomas's thought still embraced the abstract and universal principles that are so fundamental in the Aristotelian tradition. The followers of Ockham rejected these principles in favor of a science of the particular. Some of the followers of Ockham later moved on to the study of the empirical sciences.[10] Thomas also strongly defended the idea that philosophy worked hand and hand with theology. Even though he maintained that philosophy and theology are separate disciplines, he stressed the unity of the two sciences rather than their strict separation, as so many of the nominalists did.

Perhaps the most important difference between the thought of William of Ockham and that of Thomas Aquinas, however, can be seen in the former's doctrine of the primacy of the will. In the tradition of Duns Scotus, Ockham was convinced that the will is more important for human action than the intellect. By extension, if the will holds the central place in an ethical theory, emphasis will shift from the rational character of acts to law and commands. For Ockham, all law has its foundation in divine commands. Anthony Kenny has summarized this doctrine very nicely:

> Like Scotus, Ockham places law, not virtue, in the centre of ethical theory. He goes further than Scotus, however, in emphasizing the absolute freedom of God in laying down the divine law. Whereas Scotus accepted that some precepts (e.g. the command to love God) were part of a natural law, and derived their force not from the free decision of God but from his very nature, Ockham taught that the moral value of human acts derived entirely from God's sovereign, unfettered, will. God, in his absolute power, could command adultery or theft, and if he did so such acts would not only cease to be sinful but become obligatory. (II Sent. 15. 353)[11]

Clearly, Ockham's position works in direct opposition to the natural-law theory defended by Aquinas. For Ockham, a human act is right or wrong because of a divine command, not because it may or may not correspond to an appropriate nature, as is indeed the case in Thomistic natural law.

In spite of the overpowering influence of nominalism during the second half of the fourteenth and fifteenth centuries, there were important defenders of the old Thomistic system, including John Capreolus (c.1380–1444), a well-known Dominican who lectured at Paris and Toulouse.[12] The revitalization of the Thomistic spirit, however, was not fully realized until early in the sixteenth century with Cajetan

and Vitoria. Cardinal Cajetan (Thomas de Vio, 1468–1534) is probably
the most celebrated Thomistic commentator in history. Francisco de
Vitoria (c.1492–1546) is the father of Spanish Thomism. Through his
great personal influence, the *Summa theologiae* replaced the *Sentences*
of Peter Lombard as the principal text for theological study at the University of Salamanca.[13] This was the start of a movement in Spain that
would have tremendous implications. Concerning this point, Francisco
Peccorini has written,

> This would seem to be a significant event, for through his own
> teaching at Salamanca Vitoria was about to give Europe a whole
> generation of outstanding professors such as Melchior Cano
> and Domingo Soto, who in turn would pass on the Thomistic
> torch to others, such as the Jesuit Cardinal Toletus, a disciple
> of Soto, who used his influential chair at the Roman College to
> spread the word throughout the Continent. In this chain, Peter
> Fonseca, S.J., was undoubtedly one of the most effective links
> through the publication of his *Cursus Conimbricenisium* which
> he undertook while teaching at the University of Coimbra in
> Portugal and which was designed to update in a critical way
> traditional Aristotelianism.[14]

The Thomistic revival at Salamanca would bear fruit almost immediately. The great tradition initiated by Francisco de Vitoria was
characterized by great legal theorists and moral philosophers. Not sur-
prisingly, Vitoria himself was particularly interested in the *Secunda secundae* of Aquinas's *Summa*. The European discovery of the New World
would open the door for a number of new issues in moral philosophy
(and both canon and civil law) regarding the status of the peoples in
the newly discovered colonies. For this reason the School of Salamanca
is known more for its moral philosophers than for its metaphysicians.
This fact, however, should not lead us to believe that there were no
important philosophers of being in this school. Although he is now remembered most for his participation in the late-sixteenth-century controversy on Grace, Domingo Báñez (1528–1604) was an outstanding
metaphysician. Báñez was also perhaps Aquinas's most faithful commentator. In his commentary on the *Prima pars* of the *Summa* we find

the most thorough and lucid explanation of St. Thomas's philosophy of being in the sixteenth century. Báñez's commentary on question 3, article 4 provides us with an excellent example of how Béñez explains the importance of existence for Aquinas's philosophy of *esse*:

> The act of existing is something real and intrinsic to the existent, for *esse* is that by which a thing is constituted as outside nothingness. . . . Existence is the first actuality, by which a thing is posited outside nothingness, and therefore it has to be within the thing. It is unintelligible how a thing could be constituted as outside nothingness by something which is not internal to it. Furthermore, if the first actuality of a thing were extrinsic to it, then no other actuality could be intrinsic to it. The first actuality is the root of every other actuality.[15]

Few commentators before or after Báñez have understood this ontological character of Thomas's thought so clearly. Only in the twentieth century have commentators come to understand the role of existence in Thomas's thought as well as Báñez understood it.

With the focus now more on moral and legal problems, and a more careful attention paid to the *Summa*, it seemed for some time that the force of nominalism had been circumvented. In reality, the new turn that nominalism was about to take would make it an even more dominant force than it had been with William of Ockham. Indeed, centuries after Ockham's death nominalist ideas would become an essential component in the thought of many important philosophical figures. One such figure was Francisco Suárez:

> However, all this impressive anti-nominalistic effort would be overpowered and even undermined by the eclectic mind of another illustrious Jesuit, Franciscus Suarez, who joined Fonseca at Coimbra and was destined to dominate the Scholastic state for three centuries. His teaching indeed was bound to touch even a young man called René Descartes who would study at the "College de la Flèche" in Paris, and his frame of mind would impress the new philosopher thereby exerting a decisive influence on the whole Modern Philosophy.[16]

Suárez—whose honorific title, *Doctor eximius*, gives some indication of the fame he would later achieve—is, after St. Augustine and Thomas, probably the most influential figure in Christian metaphysics. His most important philosophical work, the *Disputationes Metaphysicae*, was used as the basic textbook for metaphysics in European universities for generations after the great theologian's death.[17] Although Suárez was perhaps the greatest philosopher in the Thomistic tradition, he differed profoundly from the Angelic Doctor in his metaphysics. The primacy of existence, so fundamental for Aquinas, is lost with Suárez, for whom essence and existence can both be either potential or actual, as Joseph Owens explains:

> Just as a thing like a tree or a stone can be conceived as a nonbeing before it existed and as being when it exists, so essence and the existence can each be conceived as potential and as actual. It is the proper actuality of each in its own respective order that formally constitutes the difference in all cases between a being and a nonbeing. Such is the full force of the Suarezian conception of essence and existence as things or realities (*res*). Essence is no longer simply a potency to being, and existence is no longer of its very nature actual. Like any other "things," these two, each entirely within its own order, can be considered either as actual or as potential.[18]

For Suárez, all being is reduced to essential being; existence is always subordinate to essence. Although "actuality" is important for Suárez, he does not stress the significance of the act of existence. When being is understood primarily as essence, the immediate and real character of being is lost. Existence is no longer that which makes being real through actuality. In part, Suárez adopts this conception of being because he almost always considers being as a noun rather than as a participle. This distinction is crucial for our understanding of Suarezian metaphysics:

> Taken as a participle, being signifies "the act of existing as exercised and is the same as the actual existent." Looked at as a noun, it means "the essence of a thing which has or can have existence (*esse*) and it can be said to signify existence itself not as exercised

in act but in potency or aptitude." Thus, taken as a noun, the objective concept of being is that which is or can be, that which has a real essence prescinding from actual existence without excluding or denying it.[19]

In this system, metaphysics becomes the science of possible being rather than actual or real being. As a result of this conception, being becomes fragmented:

> In short, for Suarez anything that is distinct can have an existence of its own. Matter, form, even essence and existence, must conform to this rule. This is why Suarez denies the distinction of essence and existence. Suarez makes this mistake because he takes it for granted that his *verbum mentis* corresponds exactly to what it represents, even when he uses it to conceptualize the principles of being itself. And since a mental word is by nature representative of an *ens*, itself being an act uttered according to an essence or form, all the elements Suarez admits in beings are conceived as parts—each with an essence and act all its own.[20]

Despite an extraordinary effort to resolve many of the most difficult metaphysical problems, the philosophy of Francisco Suárez is constructed on an ontological foundation that does not take into account the crucial role existence plays in our understanding of being. We see this clearly in *Disputationes Metaphysicae* XXXI, Section VI, 23:

> Therefore, it must be said that essence and existence are the same thing but that it is conceived of under the aspect of essence, insofar as by its character the thing is constituted under a particular genus and species. For essence, as we have explained above, disp.2, sect.4, is that by which something is primarily constituted within the realm of real being (*ens*), as it is distinguished from fictitious being (*ens*). In each and every particular being (*ens*) its essence is called that by whose character it is constituted in such a grade or order of beings.[21]

Although Suárez assigns some importance in his system to existence, his first consideration of being is always as an essence. In fact, for Suárez, existence is merely a further conceptualization of being. Suárez, the great synthesizer of medieval scholasticism, and in particular of the Thomistic system, does not adopt Aquinas's most fundamental ontological principle, the primacy of existence in the consideration of being.

The same point could be made regarding Suárez's notion of individuation. For him, neither matter nor existence constitute the principle of the individual. The fact that Suarez would affirm that accidents contain within themselves their own principle of individuation radically distinguishes his position from that of Thomas.[22] The argument that accidents have their own principles of individuation leads logically to the conclusion that a being contains within itself a multiplicity of individuating principles. In fact, when Suárez concludes that accidents have their own principle of individuation he breaks with the tradition of Aristotle as well as Aquinas. Ultimately, by considering substance and accidents separately, Suárez destroys the very unity that most characterizes the Aristotelian-Thomistic conception of substance. For both Thomas and Aristotle, substance and accidents must always be considered together, with substance as the controlling element and matter the individuating principle of substance. For Aquinas, it is precisely because a substance exists that its accidents cannot be considered as separate.

If it is indeed true that Thomas Aquinas was the first philosopher to develop fully a metaphysics of existence, it is certainly also clear that the Angelic Doctor was not the first to distinguish between the existence of a thing (*esse*) and that which is (*id quod est*).[23] Ralph McInerny has shown, quite convincingly, that a key moment in the history of this all-important distinction occurs in Boethius's *De hebdomadibus*. In his careful analysis of Thomas's commentary on this text, McInerny has illustrated precisely how Thomas understood the relationship between essence and existence.[24] My point, however, is not that Aquinas also made this distinction, but rather that he turned existence into the most fundamental metaphysical principle for our understanding of reality. On this foundation an epistemology and an ethics are developed. In fact, the Thomistic system can be understood as a series of logical extensions from this first premise.

Beyond the purely philosophical realm, for Thomas this knowledge can also be understood as the perception of a divinely created universe in which each individual thing receives its existence from the source of all existence, God:

> We are bound to conclude that everything that is at all real is from God. For when we encounter a subject which shares in a reality then this reality must be caused there by a thing which possesses it of its nature, as when, for example, iron is made red-hot by fire. Now we have already shown . . . that God is sheer existence subsisting of his very nature. . . . We are left with the conclusion that all things other than God are not their own existence but share in existence.[25]

Every act of perception, therefore, is in a sense a religious act, because to perceive the existence of things is to recognize the existence of God, who causes things to exist:

> Now since it is God's nature to exist, he it must be who properly causes existence in creatures, just as it is fire itself that sets other things on fire. And God is causing this effect in things not just when they begin to exist, but all the time they are maintained in existence, just as the sun is lighting up the atmosphere all the time the atmosphere remains lit. During the whole period of a thing's existence, therefore, God must be present to it, and present in a way in keeping with the way in which the thing possesses its existence. Now existence is more intimately and profoundly interior to things than anything else, for everything . . . is potential when compared to existence.[26]

In a very profound sense, philosophy, and especially ontology, is a consideration of a divinely created reality for Aquinas.[27]

For Suárez, and for so many philosophers who come after him, metaphysics becomes a science of things in themselves or a purely conceptual science of self-conscious perception. The legacy of Suárez, beginning with his students in Spain, Italy, and Portugal and lasting to our own time, is overwhelming. The author of the *Disputationes Metaphysicae* is at once the last of the great Renaissance scholastics and the father of much of what could be called modern philosophy. True knowledge of the world as it really exists (as opposed to how we perceive it) is, for most modern philosophers, no longer thought to be attainable.[28] The divinely created reality that so moved Aquinas in his philosophical speculation is later understood either in the most abstract and general way or in a very narrow "scientific" way. Eventually, the divinity of the external world is no longer a consideration; either the thinking mind itself becomes divine (Hegel), or all discussion of the divine is relegated to a nonphilosophical realm.

Chapter Two

ONTOLOGICAL MORALITY
AND HUMAN RIGHTS

Thomas Aquinas strongly defended the notion that morality is grounded in nature and being. Thomas's position is that moral action must be understood in terms of the rational nature of human beings. In this sense, nature itself is the model for moral understanding. That is to say, nature provides the principles for how things work. Although he was not, like Aristotle, a natural scientist, Aquinas did embrace a teleological view that was clearly based on the Aristotelian model. Ernest L. Fortin has described this system as follows:

The heart of the Aristotelian enterprise is the well-known and now almost universally contested thesis that nature acts for an end. This principle applies to inanimate as well as animate beings, all of which are said to be ordered to a determinate end or ends, and endowed with a constitution suited to the attainment of these ends, along with an inclination to pursue them and rest in them once they have been attained. As used in the *Physics*, nature is defined as the primary and intrinsic principle of motion and rest in beings that are subject to change, that is, beings composed of matter and form and thus capable of motion of one kind or another: local, quantitative, or qualitative. It is remarkable, for instance, that plants, animals, and human beings grow until they reach a certain size and then just as mysteriously stop growing. Mobility, the most universal characteristic of such beings, is the formality under which all of them can and must be studied. If everything around us were perfectly stationary, there would be no natural science. Only in the light of the end to which this mobility is ostensibly directed can we make sense of the regularities that we observe in the operations of nature.[1]

In the strictest sense, Thomas adopts the Aristotelian understanding of nature as a general frame of reference for his moral philosophy. Aquinas also brings this position into complete agreement with his own metaphysics, which has as its most distinctive feature the notion of existence as perfection (as we saw in chapter 1). Thus, for Aquinas, moral action must be understood in terms of the perfection of being:

> Good and bad in actions should be discussed like good and bad in things, since action springs from each thing according to the sort of thing it is. Now the degree of good it possesses matches its degree of real existence, for "good" and "being" are convertible terms. . . . Accordingly we should say that every action inasmuch as it has something real about it has something good about it; and that inasmuch as it fails to have the full reality a human act should possess then it falls short of goodness, and so is referred to as bad: thus, for example, when it fails to meet the measure of what is reasonable or is out of place or exhibits some such shortcoming.[2]

Moral principles for Aquinas are, therefore, absolute since they are based on an immutable ontological foundation. Ethical or practical wisdom is best understood not as separate from but rather an extension of speculative knowledge, as Jan A. Aertsen argues:

> Theoretical reason and practical reason are not "two branches" of knowledge. They are not distinct powers but differ only in their ends: theoretical reason is directed solely to the knowledge of truth, whereas practical reason directs truth to action. Its end is the operation. Practical reason knows truth, just as theoretical reason does, but regards the known truth as the norm (*regula*) of action. The striking term through which Thomas characterizes the relation between theoretical and practical reason is "extension": theoretical reason becomes practical only *per extensionem*.[3]

In this system, man, as a rational being, makes informed choices. His intellect guides his will. Moreover, only human beings are capable of acts of moral volition, since acts of this kind require knowledge that human beings alone can possess, as Aquinas states:

> A being of rational nature alone is capable of such knowledge. Partial knowledge of an end consists merely in perceiving it without appreciating it in terms of purpose and the adaptation of activity to that purpose. This is the sort of knowledge encountered in animals through their senses and natural instinct. Full knowledge of an end goes with voluntary activity in the complete and proper sense of the term; it is present when someone, having apprehended and deliberating about an end and the steps to be taken, can be moved to it or not.[4]

Here it is not necessary for Thomas to mention any sort of divine command. Human beings by their nature are capable of making these moral choices.

Nevertheless, Thomas had an understanding of morality quite different from most contemporary notions. The moral relativism so prevalent today would have been unthinkable to Aquinas. Thomas's view of human action is also quite different from that of Aristotle. If one can, in fact, characterize the Stagirite's moral philosophy as a virtue ethics, it can be argued that Aquinas had this in common with Aristotle. However, Thomas's moral principles lead one to a goal quite distinct from life as a "magnanimous man." Although it is difficult to determine exactly what constitutes perfect happiness for Aristotle, it is clear that happiness for him can be achieved only through a life devoted to contemplation and virtuous activity.[5] For Thomas, as a Christian philosopher, a person's ultimate happiness can only be achieved in the next life, when he or she is finally able to contemplate God's essence in the beatific vision.[6] It is not enough to be virtuous or magnanimous; human beings must live lives in accord with divine precepts. The common person learns these principles as a set of immutable rules (namely, the Ten Commandments); for the theologian, these precepts are also discerned from the careful observation of a divinely created universe. Both the common person and the theologian achieve ultimate happiness (in the next life) by living according to these principles.

We might understand this position better if we examine a fairly straightforward example. For Aquinas, homicide (which we will define as the deliberate taking of an innocent life) as a human act is indefensible. On one hand, an act of homicide is a violation of one of the Ten Commandments. Both the common person and the theologian understand this point. On the other hand, homicide is also indefensible because it constitutes a violation of the "nature" of a human being. This second argument requires a higher level of moral understanding. Aquinas addresses this specific issue as follows:

> A man can be looked at in two ways—in isolation and in some context. Now, considering man in isolation, it is not legitimate to kill any man. Every man, even the sinner, has a nature which God made, and which as such we are bound to love, whereas we violate it by killing him. It nevertheless remains true, as we have already seen, that sin corrodes the common good and so justifies the killing of the sinner, whereas the life of just men preserves and promotes the common good, since they constitute the bulk of the people. There is, therefore, simply no justification for taking the life of an innocent person.[7]

Thomas does not condemn the execution of those whose actions constitute a danger to the common good; rather, he defends the lives of innocent human beings. This position is based, first of all, on the principle that human life, as a divine creation, has intrinsic worth and must, therefore, be respected. Secondly, the "life of just men preserves and promotes the common good." The common good is important for all men because humans are social beings by their very nature. This nature is protected when innocent human beings are protected. The lives of just persons, therefore, preserve and promote the dignity of all human beings. For the common person, the commandment against killings another human being is sufficient; however, for the theologian a more complex understanding of the nature of human beings and of human society is required for one to be able to understand the indefensibility of homicide.

This notion of the dignity of the human person is not Aristotelian. While Aristotle clearly has a high regard for man as a rational being, he does not conceive of humankind as being created in the image of God. In the *Politics* we find numerous examples of the Stagirite's callous disregard for the value of human life. One such case can be found in book 7, where Aristotle defends the termination of the lives of "deformed" and unborn children:

> As to the exposure and rearing of children, let there be a law that no deformed child shall live. But as to an excess in the number of children, if the established customs of the state forbid the exposure of any children who are born, let a limit be set to the number of children a couple may have; and if couples have children in excess, let abortion be procured before sense and life have begun.[8]

Although both Aristotle and Aquinas construct ethical and moral systems on metaphysical principles, they have entirely different conceptions of the value of human life. In fact, Aristotle has no doctrine defending the dignity of the human person. For Aristotle, a child has worth only insofar as it has the potential to become a virtuous adult; it does not, therefore, enjoy in any absolute sense the same status as a mature human being. The point is evident when we consider Aristotle's argument that children cannot experience happiness:

> Since, then, happiness is a complete good and end, we must not fail to observe that it will be found in that which is complete. For it will not be found in a child (for a child is not happy), but in a man; for he is complete. Nor will it be found in an incomplete, but in a complete, period.[9]

Clearly, for Aristotle a child cannot enjoy happiness because a child is not yet a "complete" human being. The issue for Aristotle is not one of sin or innocence, but rather of nature's end. Nature must provide the principle of explanation for the most fundamental questions of reality. Within this scheme a clearly discernible hierarchy is present, as Aristotle himself explains:

Now, it is obvious that the same principle applies generally, and therefore almost all things rule and are ruled according to nature. But the kind of rule differs—the freeman rules over the slave after another manner from that in which the male rules over the female, or the man over the child; although the parts of the soul are present in all of them, they are present in different degrees. For the slave has no deliberative faculty at all, the woman has, but it is without authority, and the child has, but it is immature.[10]

One might ask why it is true that nature does not always yield a "perfect" result? For Aristotle, the answer is logically quite simple: nature sometimes commits errors:

Now mistakes occur even in the operations of art: the literate man makes a mistake in writing and the doctor pours out a wrong dose. Hence clearly mistakes are possible in the operations of nature also. If then in art there are cases in which what is rightly produced serves a purpose, and if where mistakes occur there was a purpose in what was attempted, only it was not attained, so must it be also in natural products, and monstrosities will be failures in the purposive effort.[11]

Obviously, when this doctrine is applied to the human species it has frightening implications. This is the very reason why Aristotle defends the killing of "deformed" children. For Aristotle, a "deformed" child, though innocent, constitutes one of nature's mistakes; it is, therefore, acceptable to destroy this form of imperfect life. I would argue that no credible doctrine of human rights can be based exclusively on an Aristotelian anthropology, since nature shows no compassion for the weak, the innocent, or the "deformed."

Thomas's strong defense of the human person has led some modern scholars to argue that he was, in fact, a defender of a specific set of natural human rights. This position is actually quite complex, since what we now call "human rights" was a concept foreign to Thomas Aquinas. While it is true that he did defend the dignity of the human person, this does not necessarily mean that Aquinas would have defended a positive doctrine of human rights. In a recent study of Thomas's thought, John Finnis argues that Aquinas did, indeed, defend this notion:

> Though he never uses a term translatable as "human rights," Aquinas clearly has the concept. He articulates it when he sums up the "precepts of justice" by saying that justice centrally [*proprie dicta*] concerns what is owed to "everyone in common" or "to everyone alike" [*indifferenter omnibus debitum*] (rather than to determinate persons for reasons particular to them [*ex aliqua speciali ratione*]). For, as he goes on to say, what is owed to everyone alike, in the great "republic of God" in which every human being is a member, includes at least: not to be intentionally killed by another private person, or in any other way physically [*in personam*] harmed, or cuckolded, or subjected to loss or damage of property, or falsely accused or in any other way defamed. Such a list of *iniuriae*—violations of right(s)—is implicitly a list precisely of rights to which one is entitled simply by virtue of one's being a person. Aquinas would have welcomed the flexibility of modern languages which invite us to articulate the list not merely as forms of right-violation (*in-iur-iae*) common to all, but straightforwardly as right common to all: human rights.[12]

I must take issue with Finnis on this point, however, because even though one could argue that what Thomas defends seems to be compatible with the modern notion of human rights, Aquinas conceives of justice in a sense that is quite different from the modern sense. For Thomas, human beings are not free-standing individuals. This sense of individuality is quite incompatible with Thomas's thinking. The same is true with regard to the modern notion of human freedom. Aquinas defends the dignity of the human person because he conceives of man as a rational substance created by God; he did not imagine that human beings should have the freedom to live as they choose in a human society.

In Thomas's discussion of "Precepts About Justice" (*Summa theologiae* II–II q. 122) he makes it quite clear that he is concerned with a list of negative precepts "which have a universal application" rather than with positive precepts (q. 122, art. 6). It is extremely important to note that this treatment is cast in a negative light rather than a positive one. Although Finnis uses this very passage from the *Summa* to support his argument, I think that it is clear from the text that Aquinas defends neither a positive nor a personal doctrine of human rights. Rather, throughout this entire section (question 122) he defends a doctrine of absolute responsibility to God and neighbor. In Thomas's system, *ius* or right is understood in terms of justice, which is itself always understood in terms of others:

> The proper characteristic of justice, as compared with the other moral virtues, is to govern a man in his dealings towards others. It implies a certain balance of equality, as its very name shows, for in common speech things are said to be adjusted when they match evenly. Equality is relative to another. The other moral virtues, however, compose a man for activities which befit him considered in himself. . . . So then something is said to be just because it has the rightness of justice; it is this that engages the activity of justice, even abstracting from the temper in which it is done; by contrast, the rightness of the other moral virtues is not determined apart from the frame of mind of the person acting. This is why for justice especially, in comparison with other virtues, an impersonal objective interest is fixed. We call it the just thing, and this indeed is a right [*ius*]. Clearly, then, right [*ius*] is the objective interest of justice.[13]

For Aquinas, therefore, rights are not personal; *jus* or "right" must always be understood within the context of the "objective interest of justice," because justice transcends individual rights. The common good must always be placed before the good of individuals. If a doctrine of rights is to be found in the teachings of Thomas, my view is that those rights would have to be of the negative sort rather than the positive rights defended by writers after the time of Hobbes.

In the Aristotelian corpus we do not find a treatise devoted exclusively to law; however, in his works we do find numerous passages in which he discusses this subject. From these texts it is clear that Aristotle had a strong sense of natural law. One of the most explicit statements of this conviction is found in book 1 of the *Rhetoric*:

It will now be well to make a complete classification of just and unjust actions. We may begin by observing that they have been defined relatively to two kinds of law, and also relatively to two classes of persons. By the two kinds of law I mean particular law and universal law. Particular law is that which each community lays down and applies to its own members: this is partly written and partly unwritten. Universal law is the law of nature. For there really is, as everyone to some extent divines, a natural justice and injustice that is common to all, even to those who have no association or covenant with each other. It is this that Sophocles' Antigone clearly means when she says that the burial of Polyneices was a just act in spite of the prohibition: she means that it was just by nature.[14]

It is somewhat ironic that perhaps the clearest statement made by Aristotle on this doctrine would be found in his treatise on rhetoric; however, despite the fact that the passage does not appear in a longer, more technical discussion of legal theory, we can glean a great deal from this text. First of all, for Aristotle, "particular" or positive law is quite distinct from "universal" or natural law. On this point he is in substantial agreement with Thomas. Second and more importantly, for both thinkers the question of natural law is inseparable from the issue of natural justice. This point is crucial for our understanding of both Aristotle and Aquinas.

The Dominicans who form the School of Salamanca (Vitoria, Soto, Báñez, and so on) are all followers of Aquinas in legal theory. For them, individual or human rights are always understood within the more general context of justice. Perhaps the most impressive synthesis of Thomistic principles and legal theory from this group of writers can be found in Domingo de Soto's *De iusticia et jure*. In this text we find the clearest definition of *ius* or right when Soto contrasts *ius* with *dominium*:

ius is the same as what is just (as Isidore says in Book V). It is the object of justice, the equity which justice establishes between men, dominium is the facultas of a lord (as its name implies) in servants or objects which he can use as he likes for his own benefit. Ius must therefore not be confused with dominium, as it is superior to it, and of wider reference.[15]

This distinction stressed by Soto between *ius* and *dominium* is of supreme importance for the School of Salamanca thinkers. *Dominium*, as Soto here describes it, expresses a personal control or power over a person or an object, while *ius* reflects a condition or state of equity. The two notions are quite distinct. The traditional Thomistic view is that *ius* signifies "what is just."

Some scholars are convinced that when Vitoria and Soto challenged the legitimacy of the Spanish Conquest, they were, in fact, defending the human rights of the native inhabitants of the New World. Brian Tierney, for example, has argued that Vitoria's use of the term *dominium* shows that what Vitoria was truly considering was natural rights:

> The issue concerned theologians, Vitoria explained, because the Indians were not subject to the Spanish by human law; hence, their status had to be considered in relation to divine law, presumably the divine natural law that initially conferred dominion on humankind. The subsequent discussion centered on the term *dominium* but since, as Vitoria wrote, *dominium* was nothing else but a right, his argument was essentially about rights and, insofar as he was considering natural dominion, about natural rights.[16]

If one follows this logical progression, one may, indeed, agree with Tierney, but the difference between the traditional notion of *dominium* as Vitoria understood it and a doctrine of "natural rights" is vast. The only way that Tierney's claim can be true is if we are convinced that Vitoria radically changed the doctrine defended by St. Thomas. In fact, this is precisely what Tierney tries to prove:

> Aquinas argued that law indicates what is objectively right. Vitoria took him to mean that law defines an area of subjective rights. Vitoria was relying here on a concept of permissive law that he introduced into his argument explicitly a little further on. He was treating a right as a kind of license to act within the framework

of law; for Vitoria permissive law defined an area of free choice where a person was not commanded or forbidden to act in a certain way but could say, "I use my right."[17]

Tierney's argument is that Vitoria transformed Thomas's position into a defense of subjective rights. When Tierney describes this transformation one almost gets the impression that Vitoria was defender of modern personal rights. Thus, Tierney describes Vitoria's treatment of a right "as a kind of license to act within a framework of law." Clearly, what Tierney has done with this characterization is to assign to Vitoria a doctrine of positive rights. I would argue that the issue of personal human rights had little to do with the School of Salamanca position. In fact, what these writers were defending was the legitimacy of Native American communities—that is to say, the "right" of these peoples to govern themselves in human societies. It is for this very reason that Vitoria, in his *Relectio de Indis*, devotes entire sections of his discussion to issues such as "Whether these barbarians, before the arrival of the Spaniards, had dominion, public and private" (Question I, article 1); "That our most serene Emperor might be master of the whole world" (Question II, article 1); "That the just possession of these countries is on behalf of the supreme pontiff" (Question II, article 2); or "That possession of these countries is by right discovery" (Question II, article 3). In each case, Vitoria argues that the "barbarians" were indeed the legitimate rulers of their lands. The primary issue for the Spanish Dominicans from Salamanca was not human rights, but rather legal and civil jurisdiction.[18]

In *De Iustitia et iure*, Domingo de Soto states that even if these lands were ruled by natural slaves, Christian nations would have no right to conquer them:

> And with this it should be enough to satisfy those who ask if we as Christians by virtue of the right of natural *dominium* can attack with weapons those unbelievers, who because of their primitive customs, seem to be natural slaves. We do not because of this acquire any right to subjugate these people, since their slavery does not deprive them of liberty, like those who have sold themselves into slavery or are prisoners of war.[19]

Obviously, Soto is not defending the personal rights of those who live in these distant lands as much as he is defending the natural right of those communities to exist. In fact, Soto here does not object to the notion of natural servitude. He mentions Aristotle's doctrine with no intention of renouncing it. For Soto, natural slaves are those persons who are in need of cultural formation. Soto's position is one in which natural servitude is reconciled with the traditional Christian defense of the dignity of the human person. For Soto, there is no contradiction in this position. Apparently, Soto did not believe Aristotle when he stated that barbarians who resist conquest should be hunted like wild animals:

> Now if nature makes nothing incomplete, and nothing in vain, the inference must be that she has made all animals for the sake of man. And so, from one point of view, the art of war is a natural art of acquisition, for the art of acquisition includes hunting, an art which we ought to practice against wild beasts, and against men who, though intended by nature to be governed, will not submit; for war of such a kind is naturally just.[20]

Clearly, Soto did not defend this radical doctrine of natural servitude. Soto, like Vitoria, sometimes ignores passages in Aristotelian texts that make the Stagirite seem less reasonable. Soto, who was more of a natural scientist than Vitoria, may have been even more willing to do this than Vitoria.[21]

The one "right" that Soto clearly does defend is that of self-preservation. This right is closely linked with natural inclination. Indeed, for Soto, this same right is one shared by man with the rest of nature, as Annabel Brett has observed: "The natural law in its sense as inclination dictates first and foremost the conservation by all natures of their nature, and thus the primary natural right is the right of self-conservation. All natures, including man, possess this right of their essence as such."[22]

Soto comes closest to defending a notion of personal rights in his treatment of self-defense. Annabel Brett has argued rather convincingly that in this discussion Soto has gone a step further than Vitoria, his model, on this question:

For Vitoria, a person both defends himself and forbears to do so out of his liberty, which is the same as his dominium and also his right. For Soto, a person who defends himself will do so by right, because like all creatures he has a natural right of self-conservation. But, unlike the rest of terrestrial nature, each individual man has that right as his own: it falls within his dominium and his liberty, and therefore it is free for him to renounce it if he will. A person renounces his natural right not by the exercise of (yet another) natural right, but by the exercise of liberty or self-dominum.[23]

Even in this context, however, it would be very difficult to argue that Soto is truly committed to a modern notion of human rights. His argument is that a human is a free moral agent and that in some very special cases he or she can choose not to defend himself or herself as a matter of charity. This position does not represent a radical departure from the Thomistic teaching. It would be a mistake to imagine that Soto was committed to principles of personal human rights in any modern sense. Soto seems rather to have adopted the traditional position, defending the primacy of justice and the common good rather than individual rights.

Francisco Suárez, in his 1612 publication, *De Legibus, ac Deo Legislatore*, discusses a meaning of the term *ius* that seems closer to the modern notion of a personal right:

According to the latter and strict acceptation of *ius*, this name is properly wont to be bestowed upon a certain moral power which every man has, either over his own property or with respect to that which is due to him. For it is thus that the owner of a thing is said to have a right (*ius*) in that thing, and the labourer is said to have the right to his wages by reason of which he is declared worthy of his hire. Indeed, this acceptation of the term is frequent, not only in law, but also in Scripture. . . . Accordingly, this right to claim (*actio*), or moral power, which every man possesses with respect to his own property or with respect to a thing which in some way pertains to him, is called *ius*, and appears to be the true object of justice.[24]

This passage appears near the beginning of Suárez's treatise in which he discusses several of the then current meanings of the term *ius*. It is difficult to know with certainty exactly which meaning Suárez accepted; however, it is clear from this text that this particular meaning of the term was one of those understood in Suárez's day.

It should not surprise us that Suárez does not here follow the strict Thomistic line of legal theory followed by the Dominicans at Salamanca. Suárez, though writing in the Thomistic tradition, very often took a different course than the one established by Aquinas. Suárez often begins a question with a Thomistic definition, but then widens the scope of the discussion. His use of sources, some medieval (Gratian, Isidore of Seville, Alexander of Hales), some classical (Plato, Aristotle, Cicero), still others patristic (Clement of Alexandria, St. Augustine), while very impressive in terms of range, often turns his text into a web of opposing theories that, at times, obscures his own conclusions. Suárez ends this section on *ius* and *lex* (book 1, chapter 2) by stating that he will use these two terms synonymously, thus obliterating a distinction of central importance for Aquinas. His decision to use these terms interchangeably was probably made for purely practical reasons, given the subject matter of this treatise; however, by ignoring this crucial distinction, his work ceased to be Thomistic in any strict sense.

One of the most important early modern defenders of a more personal and positive theory of rights was Hugo Grotius. We find this doctrine clearly delineated in his *De Iure Belli*:

> A legal right (*facultas*) is called by the jurists the right to one's own (*suum*); after this we shall call it a legal right properly or strictly so called. Under it are included power, now over oneself, which is called freedom, now over others, as that of the father (*patria potestas*) and that of the master over slaves; ownership, either absolute, or less than absolute, as usufruct and the right of pledge; and contractual rights, to which on the opposite side contractual obligations correspond.[25]

Although Grotius's *De Iure Belli* grew out of the Aristotelian and scholastic traditions, his discussion of personal rights represents a significant break with that tradition. As we see in the passage just cited, the language of rights changes with Grotius. When he speaks of the power "over oneself" as "freedom," the emphasis placed upon the individual is different from that of earlier legal texts. J. B. Schneewind has pointed out that while this doctrine may not be entirely new, it does represent a new focus in rights theory: "It is common to say that Grotius is one of the founders of individualism. His view of rights may or may not be an entirely innovative one. But it is through him that the idea of rights as natural attributes of individuals came to occupy a commanding place in modern European thought."[26]

We should note, however, that even for Grotius, these rights are always subordinate to the rights of civil society; that is to say, to the common good: "Legal rights, again, are of two kinds: private, which are concerned with the interest of individuals, and public which are superior to private rights, since they are exercised by the community over its members, and the property of its members, for the sake of the common good."[27] Grotius's ideas still fall within the parameters of traditional moral and legal thought even though his emphasis on the individual as a bearer of rights represents the first major change in rights theory after the time of the Spanish scholastics.

An even more explicit notion of human rights finds its beginnings in the writings of Hobbes, whose understanding of man and nature was entirely different from that of Aquinas and Aristotle, as Peter Stanlis has observed:

> Contrary to classical and Scholastic Natural Law teaching, Hobbes's man was not by nature a political animal, born without his consent into an organically developed civil society, and with no civil character apart from his common corporate nature and constitutional inheritance. Although Hobbes stressed the absolute duty of each citizen to obey the established power, his theory of sovereignty was totally subordinate as an influence to this theory of human nature, which laid the foundation for modern "natural rights."[28]

This new doctrine of natural rights would have been unthinkable for Thomas. While it is indeed true that Hobbes espoused a different conception of nature from Aquinas's, the most fundamental difference between the two thinkers is philosophical. For Hobbes, and for so many other thinkers who followed him, morality has no ontological foundation. By the time *Leviathan* first appeared in print in 1651, all but the most traditional defenders of the old Thomistic system had abandoned the ontological morality of Thomas Aquinas.

Chapter Three

THE WAR OF THE PHILOSOPHERS

Thomistic ontological morality has a long history. The battles waged over moral questions during the Middle Ages served as basic training for the wars that would be waged centuries later. If one can speak of moral debates in military terms, it might be said that the first of the great wars took place in sixteenth-century Spain. It was in Spain, after all, that the first great philosophical dispute concerning the humanity of non-Western peoples took place. In order to understand the context of these debates, however, we must first understand the philosophical ideas that were then most influential.

In recent decades, few scholars have contributed more to our understanding of Renaissance philosophical culture than Charles H. Lohr, who has devoted many years to an examination of those writers who in the period between 1500 and 1700 produced commentaries on the works of Aristotle. In 1988 a single volume appeared that included much of Lohr's previously published research.[1] This tome is an indispensable tool for anyone investigating Renaissance thought; Lohr's study provides accurate information on who these commentators were, where they lived, where they taught, and what they published. From Lohr's research we can establish, with some degree of certainty, which works of Aristotle were most commonly read and studied. This exercise is quite informative for anyone interested in European intellectual life in the age of Erasmus, Luther, Milton, or the writers of the Spanish Golden Age.

In his remarkable monograph, Lohr identifies approximately two hundred Spanish commentators. It should be noted, however, that there were scores of Spanish-American authors from the same period who were not included in Lohr's volume. The important study of Walter Redmond includes references to many of these writers.[2] When one considers that Portugal was joined to Spain for a while during this period and that Spanish political hegemony extended well into northern Europe during the sixteenth and early seventeenth centuries, it is clear that the Spanish Aristotelian tradition had an impact far beyond the borders of the Iberian Peninsula. Many of these writers traveled back and forth between Spain and the New World, while others held important appointments at the newly founded Roman College.

Lohr's research shows that Italy was the great center for Aristotelian commentators between 1500 and 1700. Indeed, the Roman College during this period was like the University of Paris in the thirteenth century. That is to say, it was a place where great scholars from all over Europe gathered to study and teach. The obvious difference is that the University of Paris in the Middle Ages was a center for a unified Catholic Europe, whereas the Roman College was a strictly Roman Catholic institution. It is also true that the University of Paris was the one great French university in the thirteenth century, while in Italy during this later period, there were several outstanding universities; Bologna and Padua immediately come to mind. Many of the greatest scholars in Europe lived and studied in Italy during this time. One such person was Juan Ginés de Sepúlveda, the most celebrated Spanish Aristotelian commentator of the sixteenth century.

Sepúlveda was born in Pozoblanco near Córdoba in about 1490. He left Spain for Italy while still a very young man. He had received the personal recommendation of Cardinal Cisneros to study in Italy.[3] Apparently, the education at the newly established University of Alcalá was not of sufficient quality for the young Sepúlveda, who had studied philosophy there for three years under the direction of Sancho Carranza de Miranda, one of the Spanish commentators whom Lohr identifies.[4] Sepúlveda soon found himself in the company of Pietro Pomponazzi in Bologna. Before long, Sepúlveda himself became famous as an Aristotelian commentator and editor. His translation of the *Politics* was for centuries the standard for that text.[5] Before his death in 1573 Sepúlveda also served as royal chronicler to Charles V, the Holy Roman Emperor. Curiously, Sepúlveda is remembered less for his Aristotelian commentaries and for his work as adviser and chronicler to Charles V than for his debate with the Bishop of Chiapas, Bartolomé de Las Casas, the "Apostle of the Indians," arguably one of the most recognized names in the intellectual history of colonial Spanish America. Las Casas was certainly the most controversial writer of his time. His writings defending the native peoples of the New World so concerned Charles V that the emperor called for hearings to settle the question of the legitimacy of the Conquest. These hearings took the form of an extended debate now remembered as the "Juntas de Valladolid," held in 1550 and 1551.[6] Las Casas would challenge the position championed by Sepúlveda on the doctrine of natural servitude—that is to say, the doctrine that some men are born to be slaves. As a faithful commentator of Aristotle, Sepúlveda was a defender of the doctrine found in book 1 of the *Politics*, in which the Stagirite very clearly defends this position immediately after proclaiming that men are by nature superior to women:

> Again, the male is by nature superior, and the female inferior; and the one rules, and the other is ruled; this principle, of necessity, extends to all mankind. Where then there is such a difference as that between soul and body, or between men and animals (as in the case of those whose business is to use their body, and who can do nothing better), the lower sort are by nature slaves, and it is better for them as for all inferior that they should be under the rule of a master. For he who can be, and therefore is, another's and he who participates in reason enough to apprehend, but not to have, is a slave by nature. Whereas the lower animals cannot even apprehend reason; they obey their passions. And indeed the use made of slaves and of tame animals is not very different; for both with their bodies minister to the needs of life. . . . It is clear, then that some men are by nature free, and others slaves, and that for these latter slavery is both expedient and right.[7]

Sepúlveda expresses the same idea in his *Democrates Alter*, a work written in the dialogue format so popular among the humanists. In the text itself, Leopoldo, one of the two characters in the work, questions Democrates, the character who speaks for Sepúlveda, about a number of the critical issues of the day, including the doctrine of natural servitude:

Leopoldo: "Do you really believe that anyone could be condemned by nature to live in slavery? After all, is not being subjected to the rule of another by nature the same as natural servitude? Do you think that the jurists, who (so many times) follow the rule of reason, are speaking in jest when they proclaim that all men are born free and that slavery was introduced afterwards by law?"

Democrates: "On the contrary, I believe that the jurists speak and act seriously and state their teachings with great prudence. Nevertheless, the interpretation that the jurists give to the notion of slavery is quite different from that of the philosophers. For the first group slavery consists in a certain adventitious condition which has its origin in the power of man, in the power of the law of nations and civil law; for the philosophers slavery is found in a certain feebleness of intellect and in inhuman and barbaric customs . . . and even though there are different forms of dominion, when the basis for this dominion is the rule of reason, it has as its foundation natural law, which, within its diversity proceeds, as the wise teach us, from one principle and natural dogma: the rule and dominion of perfection over imperfection, of strength over feebleness and of sublime virtue over vice. . . . In all of this we see clearly that it is both natural and beneficial that the soul should have dominion over the body, that reason should rule over appetite and that equality of dominion is pernicious to all. And, as the wise teach us, by this same measure and law men and animals are correctly ruled. Among animals the domesticated are superior to the wild, nevertheless, for the former it is better to submit to the rule of man, for in that way, and in no other, they survive. By the same reason, the husband has dominion over his wife, the adult over a child and the father over his son; in a word, the superior and more perfect over the inferior and less perfect. And the wise teach us that in the same way this same principle applies to all men in their mutual relations, for among men some are by nature masters and others are by nature slaves. On the one hand those who distinguish themselves by their prudence and talent, though not in physical strength, are rulers by nature, on the other hand,

> those who are feeble of intellect, even though they have the physi-
> cal strength to carry out their obligations and duties, are slaves by
> nature, and the philosophers add that for this group (the natural
> slaves) it is not only just but also useful that they should serve
> those who are by nature rulers.[8]

Obviously, this passage shows the powerful influence of Aristotle on
the author. Sepúlveda, speaking through Democrates, begins by establishing a very important distinction: that is, that the doctrine of
natural servitude is not understood in the same way by jurists as by
philosophers. Clearly, when Sepúlveda refers to "the philosophers" or
"the wise" he means Aristotle. Sepúlveda's argument, defending the
doctrine of natural servitude, based on biological distinctions, "among
animals the domesticated are superior to the wild," and the notion
that the "more perfect" is always superior to the "less perfect," is taken
straight from Aristotle's *Politics*. In the Spanish debate on this issue, the
jurists or canonists would be the defenders of the native peoples of the
New World. The position of the canonists, however, is not primarily a
consideration of the fundamental nature of human beings; it is, rather,
an argument about the legitimacy of human communities. Ultimately,
as we saw in chapter 2, the canonists defend the right of these newly
discovered societies to exist; they are not defending the personal rights
of individuals.

At Valladolid, where the famous debates were held, the panel of
judges included both canonists and theologians. Among those present
was Domingo de Soto. Included in his long list of works are several
titles that could be called Aristotelian commentaries. Charles Lohr, in
fact, lists six such works.[9] As we saw in the previous chapter, Soto was
also the author of one of the most important Spanish works on legal
theory, *De iustitia et iure*. In book 4, question 2, article 2 of that text,
Soto addresses the question of legal and natural servitude. He begins
his discussion with a statement about how men are by nature free:

> No law can repeal the law of nature: by natural law all men
> are born free . . . slavery is that by which someone is subjected
> to the rule of another against nature. And Gregory affirms the
> same thing when he states that it is against nature that some

men have dominion over others. Reason itself proves this, since man presides over all other animals because he enjoys reason and free will.[10]

Soto, however, knew that slavery as a legal practice had existed for centuries. His task was to explain how the practice had first started and how it could be justified. His answer is actually quite simple: slavery entered the world as a result of sin:

> Slavery is contrary to nature, that is to say, contrary to the first intention of nature, which would desire that all men live zealously in accord with reason. But when this first intention is lost, punishment follows, in accord with corrupted nature. And one form of punishment is legal slavery.[11]

Perhaps the best way to describe Soto's position is to say that Soto recognized that slavery was a necessary evil and a universally accepted legal practice. He was not, however, a strict defender of the doctrine of natural servitude. For Soto, the only natural slaves are those people in need of cultural formation.

The critique of Sepúlveda's ideas would be developed by many other Spanish thinkers. At Valladolid, Las Casas would argue that Aristotle had a completely different kind of "barbarian" in mind when he wrote the *Politics*. Las Casas would defend the native inhabitants of the New World as legitimate rulers of legitimate societies:

> Now if we shall have shown that among our Indians of the western and southern shores (granting that we call them barbarians and that they are barbarians) there are important kingdoms, large numbers of people who live settled lives in a society, great cities, kings, judges and laws, persons who engage in commerce, buying, selling, lending, and the other contracts of the law of nations, will it not stand proved that the Reverend Doctor Sepúlveda has spoken wrongly and viciously against peoples like these, either out of malice or ignorance of Aristotle's teaching, and, therefore, has falsely and perhaps irreparably slandered them before the entire world? From the fact that the Indians are barbarians it does not necessarily follow that they

are incapable of government and have to be ruled by others, except to be taught about the Catholic faith and to be admitted to the holy sacraments. They are not ignorant, inhuman, or bestial. Rather, long before they had heard the word Spaniard they had properly organized states, wisely ordered by excellent laws, religion, and custom.[12]

Las Casas's position almost reminds us of Soto's; that is to say, like Soto, Las Casas believes that the natural slave is one in need of cultural formation rather than one born to serve a human master. Although he was not trained in the Italian university system, as was Sepúlveda, Las Casas boldly challenged Sepúlveda's understanding of Aristotle's text. Both Las Casas and Sepúlveda try to appropriate the authority of the Stagirite in their arguments. Las Casas on several occasions tries to point out exactly what Aristotle meant in those passages about men who are slaves by nature. While it is true that Las Casas was not a professional commentator, it is immediately obvious to anyone who has examined the Las Casas texts that the Spanish Dominican knew Aristotle's *Politics* quite well. Indeed, he had to know this text well so that he could defend his position against the Aristotelians.

Neither man was ever proclaimed the winner at Valladolid, but if history is any indication of the outcome, Las Casas was the clear winner and Sepúlveda a miserable failure. After Las Casas many other writers became defenders of the native inhabitants of the New World. Sepúlveda seems to have had few allies in the following years. However, lest anyone imagine that Las Casas was the first Spanish defender of the American Indian, we must not forget two very important traditions that had a profound impact on Las Casas. On the one hand, we can not lose sight of the Spanish missionary tradition, and in particular of the importance of Antón de Montesinos, a Dominican missionary living and working in Santo Domingo at the same time as Las Casas. In 1511, Montesinos had condemned Spanish abuses in the New World. Three years later, in 1514, Las Casas himself would give up his financial interests in Santo Domingo and follow the example of Montesinos.[13] On the other hand, we must never discount the impact of the Spanish academic tradition on Las Casas, in particular, the influence of the School of Salamanca, and especially the work of the father of that school, Francisco de Vitoria.

In 1539 Vitoria delivered his *Relectio de Indis* in Salamanca.[14] In this lecture, Vitoria thoroughly examined the question as to whether or not the Spanish Crown had the right to conquer the Native Americans because of "rational insufficiency." The conclusion of Vitoria was clearly stated:

> As concerns the argument that these barbarians are insufficiently rational to govern themselves . . .
>
> 1. Aristotle certainly did not mean to say that such men thereby belong by nature to others and have no rights of ownership over their own bodies and possessions (*dominum sui et rerum*). Such slavery is a civil and legal condition, to which no man can belong by nature.
>
> 2. Nor did Aristotle mean that it is lawful to seize the goods and lands, and enslave and sell the persons, of those who are by nature less intelligent. What he meant to say was that such men have a natural deficiency, because of which they need others to govern and direct them. It is good that such men should be subordinate to others, like children to their parents until they reach adulthood, and like a wife to her husband. That this was Aristotle's true intention is apparent from his parallel statement that some men are "natural masters" by virtue of their superior intelligence. He certainly did not mean by this that such men had a legal right to arrogate power to themselves over others on the grounds of their superior intelligence, but merely that they are fitted by nature to be princes and guides. Hence, granting that these barbarians are as foolish and slow-witted as people say they are, it is still wrong to use this as grounds to deny their true dominion (*dominium*); nor can they be counted among the slaves.[15]

It is clear from this passage that the most important issue for Vitoria is that of *dominium*. For Vitoria, no matter how "slow-witted" the native peoples may be, they are still the legitimate rulers of their lands. When Vitoria states that Aristotle did not mean that men of superior intelligence have "a legal right to arrogate power to themselves over others on the grounds of their superior intelligence" he may, indeed, be stating a fact; however, Aristotle's argument was not about "legal" rights, but rather about nature. Vitoria's explication of Aristotle's position would almost have us believe that the Stagirite was not a true defender of the doctrine of natural servitude. Brian Tierney has suggested that Vitoria simply ignores this aspect of Aristotle's doctrine: "Vitoria seems to have just ignored or failed to assimilate these aspects of Aristotle's thought. In referring to the Indians' 'dominion over themselves and over other things' (*dominium sui*) he was instead deploying once more Aquinas's language of natural dominion, a dominion that Vitoria persistently treated as a right. The Spanish master had achieved the considerable feat of associating a defense of natural rights with Aristotle's theory of natural slavery."[16]

While I do not agree with Tierney's point about Vitoria treating dominion as a natural right, I do concur with his view that Vitoria clearly downplays Aristotle's doctrine of natural servitude. Obviously, Vitoria wanted to defend the prestige of the Greek philosopher. The problem with Vitoria's interpretation is that he makes Aristotle sound more like Thomas Aquinas than like Aristotle. In effect, Vitoria tries to make Aristotle a Christian defender of human dignity. Unlike Las Casas, Vitoria was not willing to condemn the Stagirite's doctrine. Despite this fact, Vitoria was, without question, the academic leader of the Spanish defense of the American Indian. His work was destined to have a great impact on almost all of those who would write about the justification of the Conquest in the next hundred years.

Another important writer and historian of the colonial period was José de Acosta. In his *De procuranda indorum salute*, presented to Philip II on January 24, 1588, Acosta includes an extensive discussion of the doctrine of natural servitude as a justification for the conquest of the New World. In his text, Acosta draws a sharp distinction between the "barbarians" as rulers and children and the insane (*amens*):

> In the end, this is what is most important: the barbarian is not so by nature, but rather by custom and education, while children and the insane are so by nature and not by education. And for

this reason, the sins committed by the barbarians cannot be punished (*animadvertere*) by anyone.[17]

Although Acosta cannot be called an Aristotelian commentator in the
strict sense, this discussion is, indeed, about Aristotle's doctrine of natural servitude. Although Acosta, like Las Casas, is remembered more for
his historical works than for his philosophical discussion of Aristotle's
doctrine, he did write this very impressive text refuting the interpretation of Sepúlveda. My point here is that some of the most important
and interesting discussions of Aristotle's ideas appeared in works other
than formal philosophical commentaries. In particular, the doctrine
of natural servitude is discussed thoroughly in works concerning the
nature of the peoples who inhabit the newly discovered lands.

In Spain there were many other writers trained in philosophy who
wrote theological pieces in which the views of Sepúlveda were attacked.
Two of the most important authors from this group were Domingo
Báñez and Francisco Suárez. Báñez was an excellent Aristotelian commentator; Lohr in fact, lists three important pieces authored by Báñez
in this connection.[18] As we saw in chapter 1, Báñez also belongs to a
line of Thomistic commentators that begins with Cajetan (Tommaso
de Vio, 1469–1536), the cardinal and General of the Dominican Order
who had served as the representative of Charles V in the encounter with
Martin Luther at the Diet of Augsburg in 1518.[19] Cajetan was an early
voice in the battle against the abuses of the Spanish Conquest. In his
commentary on *Summa Theologiae* 2, 2, q. 66, art. 8, Cajetan challenges
the notion that unbelievers can be despoiled of their goods by anyone
except their own temporal princes. Cajetan was well aware of the implications that this doctrine would have for the Spanish Crown; however,
in this matter he was quite bold in his defense of the "unbelievers."
Francisco de Vitoria knew Cajetan's text quite well; in fact, he refers to it
in his *De Indis*.[20] In his commentary on the second part of the *Summa*,
Báñez also includes a section on the justification of the Conquest. In
this text, he follows the line already established by Vitoria and Cajetan,
defending the *dominium* of the inhabitants of the New World.

More well known than Báñez is the Spanish Jesuit Francisco Suárez
(1548–1617) the celebrated author of the *Disputationes metaphysicae*,

discussed at length in chapter 1. In Suárez's *De triplici virtute theo-logica, fide, spe & charitate* (1621), a much shorter work than his well-known *Disputationes*, he takes up the question of whether or not a Christian kingdom might legitimately force a nation of non-subjects, in which pagan idolaters slaughter the innocent, to abandon the practice of idolatry:

> Concerning non-subjects, Major (on the *Sentences*, Bk. II, dist. xliv, qu. 4) and Sepúlveda (*De Fato et Libero Arbitrio*), then, have logically maintained that pagan idolaters may be forced by the Church to worship the one God and to relinquish the rites of idolatry, and that if these pagans refuse (to do so), they may justly be punished and deprived of their liberty and their kingdoms.[21]

Suárez then lists three arguments used by these writers to defend their positions:

> The first confirmation of such a view is this: if the heathen sacrifice grown men or children to their gods, they may be forcibly compelled to abandon this practice, at least on the ground of defence of the innocent; therefore, Christian princes may take the same measures towards any heathen people, on behalf of the honour of God. The second confirmation is that the Romans have been praised for the reason that they made subjects of the barbarian nations, in order to recall those nations to a better way of living. . . . The final confirmation is that certain peoples are so barbarous, so unfitted to acquire naturally the knowledge of God, that they seem fashioned by nature for a state of slavery, as Aristotle (*Politics*, Bk. I, chap. i . . .) has remarked; therefore, even on this ground, they might be forced to true knowledge and to an upright way of life.[22]

After a very elaborate explanation rejecting the first two arguments in which Suárez cites as authorities Cajetan, Vitoria, Soto, and others, Suárez responds to the third argument as follows:

> As for the saying of Aristotle quoted in the last (and third) confirmation, it would indeed be duly applicable, if there existed any

people so barbarous that they were neither united in a civil society, nor capable of exercising government. For in that case, it
would be not on the ground of religion, but on that of the defence
of humanity (so to speak) that they might be forcibly subjected to
the government of some state. But, in my opinion, no people so
barbarous have yet been found.[23]

This statement of Suárez is somewhat surprising when one considers
that he would defend this position as late as the early seventeenth century. After all, Suárez does not write about this question at the beginning of this debate, but rather at the end, when the Conquest itself
was virtually complete. It seems to be the case that Suárez defends a
position that leaves the door open for the discovery of a people that
could be called natural slaves. Suárez does not object to the doctrine
of natural servitude in principle. His argument is, rather, that no such
people has ever been discovered. This view expressed by Suárez appears
in a text published at least seventy years after Las Casas had proclaimed
in his *De unico vocationis modo* that there is only one human race: "una
denique sola species creaturae rationalis, quae in individuis suis per
universum mundum erat dispersa."[24]

Las Casas himself, however, was not opposed in any absolute sense
to the notion that some people could be true barbarians. In his *Defense
of the Indians* he addressed at length the question of which peoples
could be called true barbarians. However, even when considering the
possibility that some of the native inhabitants of the New World might
be true barbarians, Las Casas adds a human dimension to his discussion: "Again, if we want to be sons of Christ and followers of the truth
of the gospel, we should consider that, even though these peoples may
be completely barbaric, they are nevertheless created in God's image.
They are not so forsaken by divine providence that they are incapable
of attaining Christ's kingdom. They are our brothers, redeemed by
Christ's most precious blood, no less than the wisest and most learned
men in the whole world."[25]

It is precisely because all men are "created in God's image" that
they must be considered "brothers, redeemed by Christ's most precious
blood." Las Casas (who is often criticized for defending the importation

of African slaves to the New World) had a sense of the dignity of the human person that seems to be missing from the thought of Sepúlveda and the other defenders of the doctrine of natural servitude. The key to this notion of the dignity of the human person is precisely the doctrine that all men are created in God's image; without this teaching, natural servitude is more easily defended.

Melchor Cano, the brilliant student of Vitoria, would state unequivocally in his *De dominio indiorum*, "Nullus homo est natura servus," long before Suárez composed his *De triplici virtute*.[26] It is true that Las Casas was writing with a sense of urgency that is quite different from the cold, academic distance that characterizes the work of Suárez; however, Cano and his teacher, Vitoria, neither of whom ever saw the New World, were both compelled to defend a stronger position on this question than Suárez.

What Báñez and Cano have in common is that they are all conservative Thomists who lived and taught at the Convento de San Esteban in Salamanca. However, the reason these writers share a common view concerning the doctrine of natural servitude is that Thomas himself rejected this doctrine. In order to understand his view, it is probably best to take a closer look at exactly how Thomas's position on this question differed from that of Aristotle.

The obvious place to begin our inquiry would seem to be with Thomas's commentary on Aristotle's *Politics*. Here, however, we are faced with two problems. On the one hand, Thomas began a commentary on the *Politics* sometime around 1268, but never completed it.[27] We can not know with certainty why this exposition was never completed. On the other hand, and this is a much larger question, we can never really be certain how much a given commentary shows us about what Thomas himself thought, that is to say, how much of what Thomas writes is mere clarification of the original text and how much constitutes an accurate reflection of what he himself believed. In the case of the commentary on the *Politics*, Thomas's role is that of the commentator who simply explains what Aristotle's text means. Thomas seems to have been less interested in this text than in several of the others. One indication of this possible lack of interest is the fact that he completed an exposition of only the first two books of the text.[28]

An Aristotelian commentary in which we do see some of Thomas's own views expressed would be his commentary on the *Nicomachean Ethics*. In that particular case, Thomas not only intersperses some of his own views, but even, at times, attributes non-Aristotelian ideas to the Stagirite, as Harry Jaffa demonstrated long ago in his now classic study, *Thomism and Aristotelianism*.[29] In the exposition of the *Politics*, Thomas makes no attempt to show that he disagrees with Aristotle on the question of natural servitude. This fact, however, does not prove that he agrees with Aristotle on this issue; rather, it shows that the commentator understood the text and was willing to explain the meaning of Aristotle's work to his readers.

The best place to find Thomas's own views on this question is in other works, in particular the *Summa theologiae*. Here, we might begin with *Secunda secundae*, question 57, article 3, where Thomas clearly rejects the doctrine of natural servitude:

> From the bare nature of the case there is no reason for this man rather than that man being a slave. It is only when it is looked at pragmatically in its results that, as Aristotle says, it is expedient for him to be ruled by a wiser man whom he serves. Servitude, which is part of the *jus gentium*, is natural then in the second sense of our explanation, not the first.[30]

Obviously, Thomas's stance that no man is a slave by nature is different from Aristotle's. However, Thomas does agree with Aristotle that it is expedient for the wise to rule the less wise. What Thomas does in this passage is to use the authority of the Stagirite to support a part of his argument, and then defend a position which is clearly non-Aristotelian. In this particular case, Thomas agrees that men should be ruled by others who are wiser, but he does not defend the position that some men are born to be slaves. That is to say, Thomas does not defend the existence of slavery on the basis of nature, but rather for reasons of expediency. Indeed, even if slavery exists as a part of the *jus gentium*, it is because slavery is practical and not because it is natural to man.

Earlier in the *Summa* we find several other instances in which Thomas mentions slavery. In *Prima pars*, question 92, article one, we discover a few insights on this question in a passage on the nature of subjection:

> Subjection is of two kinds; one is that of slavery, in which the ruler manages the subject for his own advantage, and this sort of subjection came in after sin. But the other kind of subjection is domestic or civil, in which the ruler manages his subjects for *their* advantage and benefit. And this sort of subjection would have obtained even before sin. For the human group would have lacked the benefit of order had some of its members not been governed by others who were wiser.[31]

A close examination of this passage shows that it is quite similar to the previous text. That is to say, the same kind of argument is at work in both passages. In the first case, Thomas makes it clear that in the first intention of nature, all men are free. However, because of practical considerations some men must rule others. In this second passage we see that before the Fall, slavery, defined as a state where a ruler rules others for his own advantage (*ad sui ipsius utilitatem*), would not have existed. However, the principle of wise leaders ruling for the good and benefit (*ad eorum utilitatem et bonum*) of their subjects would have existed naturally. It is abundantly clear from both of these passages that Thomas's position on this question is quite different from Aristotle's. In *Prima pars* question 96, article four, St. Thomas returns to the question of whether or not human slavery would have existed in the state of innocence:

> The difference between a slave and a free man is that *a free man is because of himself,* as it says at the beginning of the *Metaphysics*; whereas a slave is geared to the benefit of another. So someone lords over another as a slave when he simply uses him for his own, that is the lord's purposes. And because everyone naturally values his own good, and consequently finds it grievous to surrender entirely to another the good that ought to be his own, it follows that lordship of this kind cannot but be punitive to those subjected to it. For this reason man cannot have lorded over man in the state of innocence in that sort of way.[32]

Again, Thomas uses Aristotle's authority to establish part of his argument, and then defends his own position on the question, which is quite different from the Stagirite's. Thomas uses strong language here to describe the negative state of the slave who has surrendered involuntarily to a lord who uses the slave for his own purposes. He describes this condition as "*contristabile*," translated here as "grievous." Clearly, Thomas is absolutely convinced that slavery in this negative sense is neither natural to man nor good. Thus, in the state of innocence this negative form of servitude could not have existed.

In *Prima secundae* question 94, article five, in his discussion of whether or not the precepts of natural law can be changed, we find still another example of Thomas's position:

> You speak of something being according to natural right in two ways. The first is because nature is set that way; thus the command that no harm should be done to another. The second is because nature does not bid the contrary; thus we might say that it is of natural law for man to be naked, for nature does not give him clothes; these he has to make by art. In this way common ownership and universal liberty are said to be of natural law, because private property and slavery exist by human contrivance for the convenience of social life, and not by natural law.[33]

Again, Thomas makes it clear in this text that he does not believe that human slavery exists naturally. It is very important to note that Thomas does not state that slavery should be abolished or that its existence constitutes a grave social injustice; his argument, rather, is that human slavery exists because of its usefulness for human life (*ad utilitatem humanae vitae*) and not because some men are born to be slaves.

Though not an advocate of positive rights in the modern sense, Thomas did defend a very strong notion of human freedom. One especially compelling text appears in a section on obedience in *Secunda secundae*, question 104, article five:

> Those matters in which one man is bound to obey another are outward actions involving the body. Even so, he is not bound to obey humans but God alone in regard to what belongs to the very nature of physical life, since in these matters all men are equal: for example in what concerns taking food and begetting children.

That is why there is no obligation either of slaves towards their master or of children towards their parents to obey with regard to contracting marriage, vowing virginity, or the like. In what relates to the control of human conduct and affairs, a subject is bound to obey his superiors within the limits of the authority in question—a soldier, his commander in military matters; a slave, his master in carrying out the labours of his service.[34]

Thomas's argument is that even a slave has the right to make decisions that relate to his personal life. The slave, like the soldier, must obey his superior in those matters which pertain to his service; but in his personal life, that is to say, in what relates to his nature as a human being, he is not subject to a master or a commanding officer. In fact, Thomas even declares that in these matters "*omnes homines natura sunt pares,*" all men are equal by nature. What we discover from this passage is that Thomas had a profound respect for the dignity of the human person. Individual human beings, ultimately, must answer only to God on those questions which relate to their personal lives (*homo homini obedire non tenetur, sed solum Deo*). For Thomas, the individual slave is a free human being; like the soldier, he must obey his superior, but only in those matters which fall outside the realm of his being as a human person. In this sense, Thomas, the greatest of the Aristotelian commentators, defended a position on human slavery radically different from the doctrine of the man Thomas often called simply "the philosopher." Ironically, Sepúlveda cites Thomas on numerous occasions to defend his position in his debate with Las Casas.

Vitoria, the great teacher at Salamanca, never saw his *Relectio de Indis* appear in print; his students kept copies of his lectures which are the sources for the modern editions.[35] Vitoria, who obviously had a very impressive understanding of Aristotle's works, defended a view of human freedom that reflected more his devotion to his master, Thomas, than to Aristotle.

Suárez, as we saw in chapter 1, starts from a different ontological principle than Thomas. From that point on, his philosophy is fundamentally different from that of Thomas. Suárez would have a powerful impact on European thought for centuries after the publication of the

Disputationes Metaphysicae. His massive text would later become a standard in European libraries and would function as the basic source for later philosophers who studied in the scholastic tradition.[36]

The philosophical debate concerning the nature of the native peoples of the New World was an important component in the controversy surrounding the legitimacy of the wars of conquest. The legal theory that grew out of this controversy would have a long history. The juridical treatises produced by the members of the School of Salamanca were primary sources for Hugo Grotius and, as such, had a major impact on the development of modern international law.[37] More importantly, the participants in this debate reveal two distinctly different views concerning the dignity of the human person. On one hand, the Aristotelians (lead by Sepúlveda) defended a hierarchical notion of human worth. At the top of the scale are adult men, who devote themselves to rational pursuits; at the bottom of the same scale are women, children, and peoples who can be called barbarians or natural slaves. The dignity of all human beings is not an idea that Aristotle and his followers ever adopted. On the other hand, the strict Thomists defended the idea that no one is a natural slave; all people are children of God and thus, foreign peoples, even if they believe in different gods, are human beings created by God who live in legitimate societies. This second group has a stronger conception of the dignity of the human person. Here I must strongly disagree with the views expressed by Anthony Pagden concerning Vitoria's position. Pagden has argued that while Vitoria rejects Aristotle's doctrine of natural servitude, he, nevertheless, describes the Native American as an "unreflective, passion-dominated" child:

> *De indis* effectively destroyed the credibility of the theory of natural slavery as a means to explain the deviant behaviour of the Indian. After Vitoria's analysis it was clear to all his followers that as a model, as a paradigm, it had failed dismally to satisfy the evidence it was intended to explain. Henceforth the Indian would cease to be any form of "natural man"—however that ambiguous phrase might be interpreted. He was now, whatever his shortcomings, like all other men, a being whose actions could only be adequately explained in terms of his culture. This "barbarian,"

by definition an "outsider," had now been brought "in"; "in," it
is true, at the lowest possible social and human levels: socially as
a peasant, a brutish creature living outside the discrete web of af-
filiations, patterns of behavior, modes of speech and of expression,
which made up the life of the civil man; psychologically as a child,
that unreflective, passion-dominated, half-reasoning being.[38]

While it is true that Pagden is arguing from the perspective of modern anthropology, he does not seem to understand the historical importance of Vitoria's affirmation that the Native Americans are, indeed,
men. They are not half-men or natural slaves; they are true men who
are the legitimate rulers of the lands they inhabit. Perhaps they are in
need of cultural formation, but they are still men in the truest sense of
the term. While I do disagree with Pagden's characterization of Vitoria's position, I think that his description of Sepúlveda's thought is quite
accurate. I find Pagden's analysis of the language of the *Democrates
secundus* especially convincing:

> The acerbity of this language—the use of images of inversion,
> commonly reserved for witches and other deviants, and of such
> descriptive terms as *homunculus*, which suggests not only stunted
> growth but, since *homunculi* were things created by magic, also
> unnatural biological origins, the persistent reference to animal
> symbolism, monkeys, pigs and beasts in general—was intended
> to create an image of a half-man creature whose world was the
> very reverse of the "human" world of those who by their "mag-
> nanimity, temperance, humanity and religion" were the Indians'
> natural masters.[39]

Here, indeed, we do find the description of a "half-reasoning being"
that Pagden attributes to Vitoria. Obviously, Pagden tries to minimize
the differences between two positions which are clearly quite distinct.
Sepúlveda was a humanist who defended a strict Aristotelian notion of
natural servitude. He was absolutely convinced that the Native Americans were natural slaves. Vitoria, a strict Thomist, rejects this position.
Pagden may, indeed, find the views of both thinkers unacceptable, but
it is both inaccurate and misleading to state that the two positions are

quite similar as Pagden does: "Sepúlveda's reading of Aristotle turns out in the end to be not so very far from Vitoria's own, it is difficult to see what all the fuss was about."[40] Pagden's remarks show that he is simply not concerned with the vastly different philosophical foundations of the two positions. For Pagden, the superficial similarities one finds in a few texts make the two positions virtually the same.

In later centuries much more emphasis would be placed on the freedom and rights of the individual, but in some cases (for instance, Hegel, as we shall see in the next chapter) the writers who most defend individual freedom would continue to describe non-Western peoples in the same way that Aristotelians did in this debate that took place in Spain centuries before. Only when each person is understood as a being created in the image of God is the true dignity of the human person embraced.

Chapter Four

THE MODERN WAY

The last half of the seventeenth century in Europe represents a time of great change in the history of positive human rights. Many of the most fundamental ideas that characterize modern human rights doctrine were either first formulated during this period or evolved from the great debates that began then. This is especially true with regard to religious rights. When one examines his *Letter on Tolerance* (*Epistola de Tolerantia*), drafted in Amsterdam in late 1685, it becomes clear that John Locke stresses the role of the individual in matters of religious freedom perhaps more than any thinker writing before his time.[1] For Locke, religious doctrine is less important than freedom of conscience and mutual respect. This view is based on a more modern notion of exactly what constitutes a church. Locke himself was very clear on this question: "A church seems to me to be a free society of men, joining together of their own accord for the public worship of God in such a manner as they believe will be acceptable to the Deity for the salvation of their souls."[2] Obviously, Locke was not a defender of traditional church teaching; he was, rather, one who had embraced a new way of understanding religious matters. In fact, Nicholas Wolterstorff has observed that for the last fifteen years of his life, Locke was doctrinally a Socinian, practicing an early form of Unitarianism.[3] Locke was also convinced that civil and ecclesiastical matters should remain entirely separate:

> The church itself is absolutely separate and distinct from the commonwealth and civil affairs. The boundaries on both sides are fixed and immovable. He mixes heaven and earth together,

things most remote and opposite, who confuses these two societies, which in their origin, their end, and their whole substance are utterly and completely different.[4]

This principle of separation was of fundamental importance for Locke, who also took a strong stand against religious oppression. When one considers that Locke composed the *Letter on Toleration* at a time of intense religious intolerance in Western Europe, this point is especially noteworthy. Indeed, the persecution of Roman Catholics in England had been severe since the time of Elizabeth I. In France, Louis XIV had revoked the Edict of Nantes in October of 1685, destroying any possibility of religious liberty for the Huguenots.[5]

Locke was so committed to the principle of religious freedom that he was even willing to argue that Native Americans should not be forced to accept Christianity:

No man should be deprived of his earthly goods on account of religion. Not even Americans, subjected to a Christian prince, should be robbed of life and property because they do not embrace the Christian religion. If they believe that they please God and are saved by the rites of their forefathers, they should be left to themselves and to God.[6]

I would argue that Locke's position here is a defense of human rights in the modern sense. Locke's argument, unlike that of the Salamanca jurists, is not about legal jurisdiction, but rather constitutes a legitimate defense of the personal rights of a non-Western people. This is possible because Locke understands religion as a matter of conscience and, thus, of personal freedom.

Although Locke was strongly opposed to most forms of religious intolerance, he was not, himself, favorably disposed to Roman Catholicism. For Locke, civil tolerance should not be extended to the Roman Church because of its intolerance of heretics:

These, therefore, and the like, who attribute to the faithful, religious, and orthodox, that is, to themselves, any privilege or power above other mortals, in civil affairs; or who on the plea of religion claim any authority over men who do not belong to their ecclesiastical communion, or who are in any way separated from it—these have no right to be tolerated by the magistrate.[7]

Locke was probably aware of Aquinas's position that Catholics were not obliged to accept the authority of a ruler who had been excommunicated by the Church (*Summa Theologiae* 2, 2, q. 12, art. 2). He was also surely aware of Robert Bellarmine's dispute with King James I concerning the oath of allegiance. Bellarmine, one of the most respected Catholic theologians of his time, had been asked to defend the Church's position against the English Crown.[8] While Bellarmine defended a very limited role for the pope in temporal affairs, the English monarch's position was that the Roman pontiff should have no voice in civil matters. Clearly, King James understood perfectly well that for Roman Catholics the civil and the religious are not separate orders. The traditional Catholic position is that the Church has a crucial role in civil matters. Indeed, as late as 1864, Pope Pius IX, in his encyclical *Quanta Cura*, would state:

> And, since where religion has been removed from civil society, and the doctrine and authority of divine revelation repudiated, the genuine notion itself of justice and human right is darkened and lost, and the place of true justice and legitimate right is supplied by material force. . . . But who does not see and clearly perceive that human society, when set loose from the bonds of religion and true justice, can have, in truth, no other end than the purpose of obtaining and amassing wealth, and that society under such circumstances follows no other law in its actions, except the unchastened desire of ministering to its own pleasure and interests?[9]

Obviously, Pius IX did not believe for an instant that the Church should remain separate from and have no voice in civil society. On the contrary, he believed that the Church has the responsibility to make civil society more humane and just. Locke's doctrine of the complete separation of church and state is absolutely incompatible with Roman Catholicism. It is therefore understandable that Locke could not defend religious tolerance for Roman Catholics.

The philosophical difficulty that Locke had with toleration of Catholics in his own day serves to underscore the social and political obstacles that would exist for Catholics in secular societies for centuries after Locke's death. Indeed, the legal and social discrimination against Catholics in Great Britain would only begin to be softened with the ratification of the Catholic Emancipation Act in 1829.[10] Locke may well not have been a secularist, but his principle of the total separation of the spiritual from the temporal prepared the way for modern secularism. When religion is understood as a purely personal matter, it becomes extremely difficult to tolerate religious groups that defend a doctrine of absolute truth in matters of faith and morals. Locke's goal for society was the peaceful coexistence of citizens. For Locke, it was more important that each person in society follow his or her own conscience than for anyone to defend a doctrine of absolute truth.

John Locke's emphasis on the personal is the characteristic of his thought that I would call distinctively modern. Indeed, this feature of modern thought may be the one that most distinguishes it from the earlier tradition. We can understand this point very clearly if we consider the history of ethics. From the time of Plato, ethics as the science of the good was never a doctrine of individual choice. Traditionally, ethics formed part of an ontological whole; it is only in modern thought that morality and being become autonomous:

> As a science of the good, ethics had always been more than a concern about human perfection. Almost from the beginning it had occupied the center of an all-inclusive ontology. But when modern thought reduced the good to personal or social perfection, independently of and occasionally in opposition to the whole, it deprived it of ontological depth and marginalized morality with respect to the totality of Being. Few modern thinkers avoided the pitfall of severing the person as creative principle from the rest of nature.[11]

I would argue that this separation of the individual from the whole of the community is exactly what Locke's doctrine accomplishes. In the Thomistic tradition what is most important is that the individual act in accord with the true objective of justice, which (as we saw in chapter 2) is itself always based on an ontological foundation. Locke's doctrine of human rights is non-ontological; by the time he was writing his most important works (in the late seventeenth century) the older understanding of the relationship between nature and morality had started to disappear. When Locke speaks of "nature," that term no longer has the same meaning as it had had for thinkers one hundred years before, who were still operating within an Aristotelian-teleological context.

John Locke's position, which stresses individual freedom rather than the true objective of justice or ontological morality, creates a very serious difficulty. If the personal is more fundamental than being (or that which exists), how can we establish an objective order for truth or morality? Immanuel Kant (1724–1804) tried to resolve this difficulty by adding a universal dimension to personal action and right. We see this principle clearly expressed in his *Metaphysics of Morals*: "Any action is *right* if it can coexist with everyone's freedom in accordance with a universal law, or if on its maxim the freedom of choice of each can coexist with everyone's freedom in accordance with a universal law."[12] While the individual will is extremely important for Kant, the personal must always find its place within the context of the universal. However, for Kant, right does not conform to an ontological order, but rather to a rational order. In this sense, right is purely external in the Kantian system, "just as right generally has as its object only what is external in actions, so strict right, namely that which is not mingled with anything ethical, requires only external grounds for determining choice; for only then is it pure and not mixed with any precepts of virtue. Only a completely external right can therefore be called *strict* (right in the narrow sense)."[13]

Kant is very careful to separate the notion of right from all ethical and ontological considerations because he was convinced that by keeping right separate from these considerations he could develop a more precise sense of the term: "The doctrine of right wants to be sure that what belongs to each has been determined (with mathematical exactitude). Such exactitude cannot be expected in the doctrine of virtue, which cannot refuse some room for exceptions (*latitudinem*)."[14] For Kant, this "mathematical exactness" is more important than any deeper principle of being or truth. Kant's philosophy begins with a critique of traditional metaphysical thought. This is the very reason why his doctrine of right (*jus*) is entirely deontological. The older Aristotelian-Thomistic moral philosophy is based on an ontological foundation. With Kant, the science of being is divorced from morality. The new foundation for morality becomes reason itself. Reason serves as the starting point and establishes the limits for moral reasoning. The participants in Kant's moral universe are guided by reason rather than by nature. Individual human beings act in accord with universal principles rather than through a sense of natural or intrinsic good.

While Kant limited the notion of right to the external and rejected an ontological foundation for right, he was, nevertheless, a strong defender of certain human rights. Unlike so many thinkers who had come before him, Kant was also a strong opponent of the doctrine of natural servitude. In part, this opposition is based on his powerful notion of human freedom:

> *Freedom* (independence from being constrained by another's choice), insofar as it can coexist with the freedom of every other in accordance with a universal law, is the only original right belonging to every man by virtue of his humanity.—This principle of innate freedom already involves the following authorizations, which are not really distinct from it (as if they were members of the division of some higher concept of right): innate *equality*, that is, independence from being bound by others to more than one can in turn bind them; hence a human being's quality of being *his own master* (*sui iuris*), as well as being a human being *beyond reproach* (*iusti*), since before he performs any act affecting rights he has done no wrong to anyone; and finally, his being authorized to do to others anything that does not in itself diminish what is theirs.[15]

The fact that he would defend the notion that every human being is equal, "beyond reproach" and "his own master" shows us that Kant was indeed a strong defender of human freedom. However, this defense of human freedom is not based on the ontological dignity of the human person, but rather, at least in part, on the formal principle that a man who has broken no law can not be treated as a criminal. We see this point clearly established in Kant's discussion of the natural rights of children: "But children (even those of someone who has become a slave through his crime) are at all times free. For everyone is born free, since he has not yet committed a crime."[16] Kant was even willing to defend the position that these same children are entitled to formal education,

> and the cost of educating him until he comes of age cannot be accounted against him as a debt that he has to pay off. For the slave would have to educate his children if he could, without charging them with the cost of their education, and if he cannot the obligation devolves on his possessor.[17]

In this particular case, Kant's position sounds almost like that of a modern human rights advocate. However, his defense of these rights (like that of so many other defenders of the "rights of man") is based on strictly formal considerations. For Kant, the notion of right is first of all a matter of law and punishment; therefore, a child is free because it has not yet broken any of society's laws. In fact, Kant goes as far as to call obedience to penal law a "categorical imperative":

> The law of punishment is a categorical imperative, and woe to him who crawls through the windings of eudaimonism in order to discover something that releases the criminal from punishment or even reduces its amount by the advantage it promises, in accordance with the Pharisaical saying, "It is better for one man to die than for an entire people to perish." For if justice goes, there is no longer any value in human beings living on the earth.[18]

One cannot underestimate the importance of this last point. For Kant, the unconditional obedience to the laws of society is the very principle that holds the state together, as Gottfried Dietze has observed:

> Kant makes plain that categorical imperatives also require obedience to positive laws. The state possesses autonomy. It creates and sustains itself with legislative, executive, and judicial powers according to laws of freedom. It profits from "the greatest conformity of the constitution with principles of law . . . the striving for which reason demands through a categorical imperative."

While the state forms itself according to the moral law, it may for its preservation require obedience to positive laws. Thus positive criminal law must be obeyed unconditionally.[19]

Since Kant understands right primarily as a matter of law and punishment, law itself is strongly tied to the notion of retribution. Kant is quite explicit about this in his discussion of capital punishment: "even if a civil society were to be dissolved by the consent of all its members . . . the last murderer remaining in prison would first have to be executed, so that each has done to him what his deeds deserve and blood guilt does not cling to the people for not having insisted upon this punishment."[20] It is precisely for this reason that Kant defends the position that all murderers should be put to death: "Accordingly, every murderer—anyone who commits murder, orders it, or is an accomplice in it—must suffer death; this is what justice, as the idea of judicial authority, wills in accordance with universal laws that are grounded a priori."[21] Clearly, Kant defends a hard-line position on this question; this is so because for Kant, matters of justice must have a universal application. The fact that an accomplice in a murder might have a very limited role means little to Kant, who is not primarily concerned with the lives of individual human beings, but rather with the survival of the community as a whole. In some instances the sovereign may show mercy and impose a lesser sentence, but this action must be done only in isolated cases with the goal of preserving the state.

For Kant, morality itself is primarily a consideration of what can be commanded. In his impressive critique of Kantian ethics, Max Scheler stresses this limitation:

Here we must reconsider in another respect the basic errors of imperativistic ethics: Only what can be commanded or prohibited is of moral value. Anything that cannot be commanded or prohibited is of no moral value, because man does (or does not do) it of his own accord, or because the acts concerned—e.g., the acts of faith and love—are such that they cannot be commanded or prohibited. These propositions are comprehensible only in light of a pragmatistic attitude which admits moral values only to the extent that man can *intervene* in the moral world and *change* it through *orders*.[22]

It is clear that what begins as the defense of personal freedom in Locke is transformed by Kant into a system of absolute imperatives, in which the personal becomes the universal. Perhaps the best way to understand this transformation is to imagine that while Locke "freed" the individual from tradition, Kant made the now autonomous individual, through a set of rational principles, the foundation of justice and right. More than any other innovation in his moral philosophy the feature that most characterizes Kant's thought is this emphasis on autonomy, as J. B. Schneewind explains: "At the core of the moral philosophy of Immanuel Kant (1724–1804) is the claim that morality centers on a law that human beings impose on themselves, necessarily providing themselves, in doing so, with a motive to obey. Kant speaks of agents who are morally self-governed in this way as autonomous."[23] This notion of moral autonomy may well be one of the most important developments in the history of modern ethics. Indeed, this doctrine is one of the features that most characterizes the thinking we now call "modern." Those who embrace the older worldview must reject this idea out of hand.[24]

It is almost ironic that a thinker who stressed duty, compliance, and responsibility as much as Kant could have been responsible for such an important break with traditional moral philosophy. Nevertheless, Kant, who was neither an Aristotelian nor an empiricist, empowered the individual will by separating practical reason from an ontological order. Indeed, this separation forms the core of the problem with Kant's moral thinking, as Henry B. Veath has shown:

> So long as Kant is either unwilling or unable to recognize the possibility that a natural desire may nonetheless be a reasoned desire and thus determined by nothing less than a knowledge of the good, he must renounce altogether any and all attempts to provide an ontological basis for ethics in terms of a thing's nature, be it human nature or the nature of rational beings generally. But the question returns to plague the Kantians more persistently than ever: how can one possibly come to know the moral laws that are incumbent upon us as rational beings if appeal is not to

be made to the nature of such beings by way of support? So far as we have been able to determine, the only way that a Kantian can answer this question is by attempting to appeal not to the nature of rational beings, but rather to the purely formal requirements that presumably must attach to moral laws, insofar as these laws are held to be binding on all rational creatures.[25]

If Descartes made the human mind the starting point for philosophical reflection, Kant made reason the foundation for ethical and moral thought. In his effort to establish a more exact and scientific science of right, Kant prepared the way for much of modern deontological morality.[26]

Born less than a hundred years after Locke's death, Georg Wilhelm Friedrich Hegel (1770–1831), may well have been the philosopher who took the argument concerning right (*jus*) to the next level. Indeed, if Hegel, like Kant, stressed the rational and the universal, he also made the self-conscious, free individual the starting point of any discussion about right:

> The human being, in his immediate existence [*Existenz*] in himself, is a natural entity, external to his concept; it is only through the *development* [*Ausbildung*] of his own body and spirit, *essentially* by means of *his self-consciousness comprehending itself as free*, that he takes possession of himself and becomes his own property as distinct from that of others. Or to put it the other way around, this taking possession of oneself consists also in translating into *actuality* what one is in terms of one's concept.[27]

In the Hegelian system, reason is no longer merely conceptual or static; the rational becomes the actual. This is precisely how Hegel was able to bridge the gap left open by Kant between the natural world and the conceptual. Hegel's system brings both orders together within the domain of the rational. In terms of individual human beings, freedom and self-consciousness become far more important than nature or the mere *concept* (Hegel's term) of the human being. Perhaps the best illustration of this doctrine can be found in Hegel's discussion of slavery in his *Philosophy of Right*:

The claim that slavery is absolutely contrary to right is firmly tied to the *concept* of the human being as spirit, as something free *in itself*, and is one-sided inasmuch as it regards the human being as *by nature* free, or (and this amounts to the same thing) takes the concept as such as its immediacy, not the Idea, as the truth. . . . The free spirit consists precisely in not having its being as mere concept or *in itself*, but in overcoming [*aufheben*] this formal phase of its being and hence also its immediate natural existence, and in giving itself an existence which is purely its own and free. That side of the antinomy which asserts the concept of freedom thus has the advantage that it contains the absolute starting point—though only the starting point—on the way to truth, whereas the other side, which goes no further than conceptless existence, does not contain the point of view of rationality and right at all. The point of view of the free will, with which right and the science of right begin, is already beyond the false [*unwahren*] point of view whereby the human being exists as a natural being and as a concept which has being only in itself, and is therefore capable of enslavement.[28]

In Hegel's view, we are not born free as human beings. We become free only through our own rationality. The human person has no ontological dignity that necessarily and absolutely requires that all men be born free. Our natural existence is of lesser importance for Hegel, for whom the rational is preeminent. No human being is born free in this system; he or she acquires freedom through rational self-consciousness.

The importance of individual free choice cannot be stressed enough in Hegel's system. For Hegel, freedom is always a matter of choice. However, despite the enormous importance that Hegel assigns to human freedom, this freedom in and for itself is not of the highest order. In order for human freedom to acquire even more importance it must serve a higher purpose and, therefore, must have a more universal end. In Hegel's *Philosophy of Right* this end is the state:

The state is the actuality of concrete freedom. But *concrete freedom* requires that personal individuality [*Einzelheit*] and its particular interests should reach their full *development* and gain *recognition of their right* for itself (within the system of the family and of civil society), and also that they should, on the one hand, *pass over* of their own accord into the interest of the universal, and on the other, knowingly and willingly acknowledge this universal interest even as their own *substantial spirit*, and actively pursue it as their *ultimate end*.[29]

Human dignity, for Hegel, must be acquired through a process of self-awareness in the state. The notion of the dignity of the human person as such, independent of the state, is a doctrine not defended by Hegel. If the "ultimate end" of human beings is only fully realized in the state, no individual human being can ever achieve this end outside of the state. The state is, therefore, the context within which human beings acquire dignity.

The view that the highest end for the human person is a religious end is strongly rejected by Hegel. For Hegel, religion provided the foundation for the modern state, which has been transformed into the direct reflection of the divine will:

> If, then religion constitutes the foundation which embodies the ethical realm in general, and, more specifically, the nature of the state as divine will, it is at the same time only a foundation; and this is where the two (i.e., the state and religion) diverge. The state is the divine will as present spirit, unfolding as the actual shape and organization of a world.[30]

Hegel's argument is rooted in history. He argues that at an earlier time the Church represented a higher level of spirituality than did the state. The modern state, however, is the new embodiment of ethical rationality:

> We do indeed know from history that there have in the past been periods and conditions of barbarism in which all higher spirituality had its seat in the Church, while the state was merely a secular regime of violence, arbitrariness, and passion. . . . But to claim that this situation is the one which truly corresponds to the Idea is to proceed too blindly and superficially. On the contrary, the development of this Idea has established the truth (of

the proposition) that spirit, as free and rational, is inherently (*an sich*) ethical, that the true Idea is actual rationality, and that it is this rationality which exists as the state.[31]

Hegel believed strongly that reality is understood most completely as the development of the rational. In the course of this development, the Church had an important role at an earlier time; however, with the further development of the rational, the state has become the embodiment of the rational, and therefore, of the ethical as well.

Ultimately, Hegel was convinced that all of world history could be understood in terms of the unfolding of an absolute rational spirit. The temporal, the spiritual, and the personal are all absorbed into the larger realm of spirit. In this system, only those European peoples who have reached the highest level of rational self-awareness can participate in the highest expression of spirit. For Hegel, non-European peoples who have not yet reached this level of rational self-consciousness do not possess the same dignity as Europeans. Perhaps the best indication of Hegel's regard for non-Europeans is found in his observations concerning world history. Here we discover that for Hegel, some peoples must be considered races of barbarians. This is clearly the case with Hegel's description of African peoples:

> All our observations of African man show him as living in a state of savagery and barbarism, and he remains in this state to the present day. The negro is an example of animal man in all his savagery and lawlessness, and if we wish to understand him at all, we must put aside all our European attitudes. We must not think of a spiritual God or of moral laws; to comprehend him correctly, we must abstract from all reverence and morality, and from everything which we call feeling. All this is foreign to man in his immediate existence, and nothing consonant with humanity is to be found in his character.[32]

Indeed, for Hegel, moral law and religion are both reflections of a spirit that manifests itself as the gradual but absolute development of self-conscious rationality. African man, unaware of this process, and therefore a slave to his own existence (according to Hegel), cannot participate in this development. So convinced was Hegel of his observations, that he argued that Africans are incapable of advanced political rule:

> If we now turn to the elements of the political constitution, we must realise that the whole nature of Africa is such that there can be no such thing as a constitution. The government must necessarily be patriarchal in character. The main characteristic of this patriarchal phase is the arbitrary rule of the senses, the energy of the sensuous will; in this arbitrary state, ethical relationships of an essentially universal content—i.e. those which take no account of the consciousness in its individual aspect, but see its value as residing in its inner universality (whether in legal, religious, or ethical contexts)—are as yet completely undeveloped. Where this universal quality is weak or remote, the political union cannot be that of a state governed by free rational laws.[33]

For Hegel, the notion of a political constitution is impossible for peoples who live exclusively with the realm of "the arbitrary rule of the senses." Thus, Hegel argues that African peoples are ruled by a "sensuous will" rather than by "rational laws." The legal, the ethical, and the universal, the unmistakable marks of peoples that have reached the highest level of rational development, are absent from African culture. Finally, Hegel declared that among African peoples, cultural development was impossible:

> The condition in which they live is incapable of any development or culture, and their present existence is the same as it has always been. In the face of the enormous energy of sensuous arbitrariness which dominates their lives, morality has no determinate influence upon them. Anyone who wishes to study the most terrible manifestations of human nature will find them in Africa. The earliest reports concerning this continent tell us precisely the same, and it has no history in the true sense of the word.[34]

Historical and cultural development are possible only in societies where the rational has overcome this "enormous energy of sensuous arbitrariness." Hegel was absolutely committed to this notion. He was also convinced that human freedom (in the true sense of rational self-consciousness) could be achieved only within the context of the modern European state.

It is almost shocking to see how similar Hegel's language is to that of Juan Ginés de Sepúlveda and the defenders of the doctrine of natural servitude in sixteenth-century Spain. In both cases, the fundamental argument is that the "natural barbarians" benefit from their contact with European civilization. In the New World, the "barbarians" must be conquered so that they can become proper Christian subjects. For Hegel, the Africans who are captured and sold as slaves in Europe benefit from the experience, since they are able to leave, if only in a very limited sense, a world of "sensuous arbitrariness."

The question that must be asked at this point is, what happened to the doctrine of the dignity of the human person? In fact, this question was already answered by Hegel in his discussion of slavery. For Hegel, human beings by their very nature do not have intrinsic worth. In principle, this argument is not unlike that of Aristotle with regard to happiness. In Aristotle's system, as we saw in chapter 2, only a mature adult is truly capable of happiness, because the exercise of rational contemplation and a life of magnanimous virtue are requirements for true happiness. This is why Aristotle clearly stated that a child is incapable of happiness. In Hegel's world, it is not just the child who is incapable of this higher state; the races of people that have not yet reached a level of development that would allow them to experience self-conscious freedom are also excluded.

Although Kant's doctrine may have differed from Hegel's in many fundamental ways, his emphasis on the universality of reason and moral autonomy prepared the way for Hegel's rational spirit. Locke, who most probably would have rejected much of what Hegel would later write, also prepared the way for Hegel with his emphasis on individual freedom. All three of these thinkers broke with the older tradition of ontological morality, that by Hegel's day had few intellectual defenders. Indeed, not since the time of the great Aristotelians of the seventeenth century had the old system found a strong enough advocate to defend it against the philosophical voices that now dominated European intellectual life.

Chapter Five

POPE LEO XIII AND HIS LEGACY

Although it would be wrong to imagine that there were not many philosophical currents vying for ascendancy in the first decades of the nineteenth century, it is clear from the previous chapter that empiricism, Kantianism, and Hegelianism were among the leading competitors. These three schools had by that time become so dominant that no philosophy within Catholic tradition could stand against them as a viable alternative. While some thinkers in Catholic circles rejected all philosophical thought that challenged the truth of revealed religion or the magisterium of the Church, others tried to incorporate the ideas of the leading "secular" philosophers into new and at times unorthodox theological systems. Two examples of this later approach are Georg Hermes, who developed a theology based on Kantian principles, and Anton Günther, whose system was inspired by Kantian and Hegelian ideas. The works of both authors were later placed on the Roman Index.[1] There were also official pronouncements condemning a series of "current errors." The best example of this kind of declaration would be the *Syllabus of Errors*, which appeared in 1864.[2] The hostile intellectual climate of the First Vatican Council is perhaps best understood in terms of the principles of the *Syllabus*.[3] Obviously, the Church was at war with a number of modern social and political trends, including liberalism and secularism.

It is within this historical context that Vincenzo Gioacchino Pecci (1810–1903), later Pope Leo XIII (1878–1903), emerges. In the history of Thomism, no figure in the nineteenth century looms larger than Leo XIII. On August 4, 1879, Pope Leo presented the encyclical letter *Aeterni Patris*, without question the most important statement made by a Roman pontiff concerning Christian philosophy in the nineteenth century. A close examination of *Aeterni Patris* reveals that Pope Leo was deeply concerned about the intellectual climate of his day. The encyclical, which has as its subject matter the restoration of Christian philosophy, begins with a sharp attack on the negative influence that secular philosophy has had on civil matters:

> Whoso turns his attention to the bitter strifes of these days and seeks a reason for the troubles that vex public and private life must come to the conclusion that a fruitful cause of the evils which now afflict, as well as those which threaten, us lies in this: that false conclusions concerning divine and human things, which originated in the schools of philosophy, have now crept into all the orders of the State, and have been accepted by the common consent of the masses.[4]

Leo, himself a man of deep learning and vast culture, was convinced that a sound philosophy could provide the foundation for a healthy state:

> For, since it is in the very nature of man to follow the guide of reason in his actions, if his intellect sins at all his will soon follows; and thus it happens that false opinions, whose seat is in the understanding, influence human actions and pervert them. Whereas, on the other hand, if men be of sound mind and take their stand on true and solid principles, there will result a vast amount of benefits for the public and private good.[5]

The philosophy that Leo proposed for this supremely important task was Christian philosophy. In simple terms, "Christian philosophy," as Leo understood it, is philosophy guided by revelation. Leo saw absolutely no contradiction in this approach to philosophical inquiry. In fact, he believed that faith could guide reason and that this philosophy would strengthen faith. The Roman pontiff even goes as far as to say that Christian philosophy is the best possible philosophy, since the light of revealed truth contributes to the "nobility" and "keenness" of philosophy:

> Those, therefore, who to the study of philosophy unite obedience to the Christian faith, are philosophizing in the best possible way;

for the splendor of the divine truths, received into the mind, helps the understanding and not only detracts in nowise from the dignity, but adds greatly to its nobility, keenness and stability.[6]

Leo had a very specific philosophical tradition in mind when he argued for the restoration of Christian philosophy; for Leo, the most "noble and admirable" philosophy was scholasticism. Within that particular school, Leo was especially impressed with the philosophy of Thomas Aquinas:

> Among the Scholastic Doctors, the chief and master of all towers Thomas Aquinas, who, as Cajetan observes, because "he most venerated the ancient doctors of the Church, in a certain way seems to have inherited the intellect of all." The doctrines of those illustrious men, like the scattered members of a body, Thomas collected together and cemented, distributed in wonderful order, and so increased with important additions that he is rightly and deservedly esteemed the special bulwark and glory of the Catholic faith.[7]

When Leo discusses Thomas's contribution to philosophy, it is clear that the Roman pontiff is describing the perfect philosopher:

> Philosophy has no part which he did not touch finely at once and thoroughly; on the laws of reasoning, on God and incorporeal substances, on man and other sensible things, on human actions and their principles, he reasoned in such a manner that in him there is wanting neither a full array of questions, nor an apt disposal of the various parts, nor the best method of proceeding, nor soundness of principles or strength of argument, nor clearness and elegance of style, nor a facility for explaining what is abstruse.[8]

Indeed, so impressed was Leo with the thought of Thomas Aquinas that he was convinced that the principles established by Thomas could guide Christian philosophers in their search for solutions to problems that would arise in the centuries after the saint's death:

> Moreover, the Angelic Doctor pushed his philosophic inquiry into the reasons and principles of things, which, because they are

most comprehensive and contain in their bosom, so to say, the seeds of almost infinite truths, were to be unfolded in good time by later masters and with goodly yield. And as he also used this philosophic method in the refutation of error, he won this title to distinction for himself: that, single-handed, he victoriously combated the errors of former times, and supplied invincible arms to put those to rout which might in after-times spring up.[9]

Leo continues with a series of remarks about how a return to the teachings of Thomas Aquinas could also provide the principles for a more complete understanding of a number of current political and social questions:

For, the teachings of Thomas on the true meaning of liberty, which at this time is running into license, on the divine origin of all authority, on laws and their force, on the paternal and just rule of princes, on obedience to the higher powers, on mutual charity one toward another—on all of these and kindred subjects—have very great and invincible force to overturn those principles of the new order which are well known to be dangerous to the peaceful order of things and to public safety.[10]

Leo concludes his encyclical with a call to arms, calling for the implementation of Thomistic doctrine in Catholic schools and universities. He also is careful to point out that this doctrine should be the authentic teaching of Thomas, taken from the works of the Angelic Doctor himself:

Let carefully selected teachers endeavor to implant the doctrine of Thomas Aquinas in the minds of students, and set forth clearly his solidity and excellence over others. Let the universities already founded or to be founded by you illustrate and defend this doctrine, and use it for the refutation of prevailing errors. But, lest the false for the true or the corrupt for the pure be drunk in, be ye watchful that the doctrine of Thomas be drawn from his own fountains, or at least from those rivulets which, derived from the very fount, have thus far flowed, according to the established agreement of learned men, pure and clear; be careful to guard the minds of youth from those which are said to flow thence, but in reality are gathered from strange and unwholesome streams.[11]

The influence of *Aeterni Patris* would be difficult to overestimate. It is not an exaggeration to state that much of twentieth-century Thomistic philosophy, either directly or indirectly, has as its point of departure this powerful encyclical. What Leo did, in effect, was to alter the course of Catholic thought. After the appearance of *Aeterni Patris*, Thomism quickly eclipsed many of the philosophical currents that were so influential in Catholic circles in the nineteenth century—for example, "Ontologism," a system based primarily on the doctrine that all human knowledge implies an immediate intuition of God. Leo was primarily responsible for this major change, but it would be a mistake to assert that he established or created a new philosophical school. What Leo did, in fact, was to proclaim Thomism the official philosophy of Catholic teachers. Thomism, as such, had been undergoing a revival in Italy since the early days of the nineteenth century. Vincenzo Buzzetti (1778–1824), one of the principal initiators of the revival, had learned Thomism at the Alberoni College in Piacenza. Later, while teaching the *Summa* at Perugia, he taught both Serafino and Domenico Sordi, important Thomists who would later become the teachers of Giuseppe Pecci and his brother, Vincenzo.[12] The brothers Sordi were members of the Society of Jesus, which had been restored in 1814. It should be noted that the nineteenth-century revival of Thomism in Italy was primarily the work of the Jesuits. Along with Serafino and Domenico Sordi, Luigi Taparelli d'Azeglio, the first director of the Collegio Romano after it had been returned to the Jesuits, would greatly influence the Pecci brothers.[13] Taparelli was also very interested in natural law, a subject that was sometimes quite controversial during this period. Because of his stand on certain social questions, Taparelli was exiled by the Bourbon regime in Naples and sent to Sicily in 1833. Domenico Sordi was also forbidden to teach natural law at the same time.[14]

Much more famous than Taparelli and the brothers Sordi were the Jesuits Joseph Kleutgen and Matteo Liberatore, both of whom were extremely important advisers for Leo. Several influential Jesuits wrote articles for *Civiltà Cattolica*, a journal that had been founded in 1849.[15] This same group was later responsible for making Thomistic philosophy mandatory in Jesuit seminaries, as Gerald A. McCool has observed:

> By 1853 Matteo Liberatore had joined the team of Jesuits on Civiltà Cattolica and Joseph Kleutgen, of the Jesuit-directed German College, was working closely with them. Taparelli's postulate that the doctrine of St. Thomas be restored as a principle of unity in the teaching of the Society of Jesus was adopted at the Society's general congregation in 1854. In 1858 Liberatore, Taparelli, Sordi, Curci, and Kleutgen prepared an Ordinatio Studiorum, incorporating their ideas, which the general, Peter Beckx, made mandatory for the Society of Jesus.[16]

Along with the Dominican, Tommaso Zigliara, all of these philosophers greatly influenced the pope. Long before *Aeterni Patris* was drafted, Leo had spent years studying the works of St. Thomas and the texts of the nineteenth-century neo-Thomists. Some of these philosophers would even help with the preparation of *Aeterni Patris*.[17]

The teachings of Thomas provide the philosophical foundation for Leo's social and political doctrine. Indeed, it would not be an exaggeration to state that in Leo's social and political thought we find a step-by-step application of Thomistic principles. A very clear example of this approach is the Roman pontiff's discussion of law in the June 20, 1888 encyclical, *Libertas*:

> Law is the guide of man's actions; it turns him toward good by its rewards, and deters him from evil by its punishments. Foremost in this office comes the natural law, which is written and engraved in the mind of every man and this is nothing but our reason, commanding us to do right and forbidding sin. Nevertheless, all prescriptions of human reason can have force of law only inasmuch as they are the voice and interpreters of some higher power on which our reason and liberty necessarily depend. For, since the force of law consists in the imposing of obligations and the granting of rights, authority is the one and only foundation of all law—the power, that is, of fixing duties and defining rights, as

also of assigning the necessary sanctions of reward and chastise-
ment to each and all of its commands. But all this, clearly, cannot
be found in man, if, as his own supreme legislator, he is to be the
rule of his own action. It follows, therefore, that the law of nature
is the same thing as the eternal law, implanted in rational creatures, and inclining them to their right action and end; and can
be nothing else but the eternal reason of God.[18]

The Thomistic influence on this text is obvious. What Leo has done
with his source is to modify it somewhat, making it applicable to the
pope's own day. Although Thomas never refers specifically to "the law
of nature," the relationship between eternal, natural, and human law
described in this encyclical is based on Thomas's *Treatise on Law* in the
Summa Theologiae.[19]

Leo strongly defends the notion that all law and freedom come from
God; therefore, he adamantly opposes any doctrine that considers men
free and independent of God's law. For this very reason, the pope was
especially opposed to liberalism:

Man, by a necessity of his nature, is wholly subject to the most
faithful and ever-enduring power of God . . . as a consequence,
any liberty, except that which consists in submission to God and
in subjection to His will, is unintelligible. To deny the existence
of this authority in God, or to refuse to submit to it, means to act,
not as a free man, but as one who treasonably abuses his liberty;
and in such a disposition of mind the chief and deadly vice of
liberalism essentially consists.[20]

The modern reader may be surprised to discover that Pope Leo
was a severe critic of liberalism. It must be remembered, however,
that this doctrine had already been condemned explicitly by Pius IX
in the *Syllabus of Errors* of 1864.[21] We should note also that Leo's
social teachings are based on a philosophical foundation that gives
primacy to absolute and immutable truth. If one's first concern is
with truth, there can be little tolerance for what is false. Under no
circumstances would Leo have defended the notion that it is perfectly legitimate to allow the printing of falsehoods in the name of

freedom. Nor would he have imagined that religion was a matter of personal choice. Therefore, it should not surprise us that Leo was not a defender of many of the basic freedoms or "rights" that are central in modern democracies:

> From what has been said it follows that it is quite unlawful to demand, to defend, or to grant unconditional freedom of thought, of speech, or writing, or of worship, as if these were so many rights given by nature to man. For, if nature had really granted them, it would be lawful to refuse obedience to God, and there would be no restraint on human liberty.

Leo, however, was a realist who understood that certain freedoms are necessary in modern societies. He was, therefore, willing to tolerate some of these modern rights, but only in moderation and with great caution:

> It likewise follows that freedom in these things may be tolerated wherever there is just cause, but only with such moderation as will prevent its degenerating into license and excess. And, where such liberties are in use, men should employ them in doing good, and should estimate them as the Church does; for liberty is to be regarded as legitimate in so far only as it affords greater facility for doing good, but no farther.[22]

The modern notion of positive rights was not completely acceptable to Pope Leo; he only begrudgingly would have agreed to a very limited set of positive rights. For Leo, only those who obey God and follow his commands are free men:

> From this it is manifest that the eternal law of God is the sole standard and rule of human liberty, not only in each individual man, but also in the community and civil society which men constitute when united. Therefore, the true liberty of human society does not consist in every man doing what he pleases, for this would simply end in turmoil and confusion, and bring on the overthrow of the State; but rather in this, that through the injunctions of the civil law all may more easily conform to the prescriptions of the eternal law.[23]

The liberal, who defends freedom of speech, thought, the press, and religion, is a slave in Leo's eyes, since this doctrine ignores God, gives equal consideration to truth and falsehood, and leads inevitably to "turmoil and confusion."

Leo did not believe for an instant (as did Kant and Hegel) that man's highest good was achieved in civil society. For this very reason he adamantly defended the notion that our allegiance to God and to the Church must always come before any loyalty to the state:

> It is a high crime indeed to withdraw allegiance from God in order to please men, an act of consummate wickedness to break the laws of Jesus Christ, in order to yield obedience to earthly rulers, or, under pretext of keeping the civil law, to ignore the rights of the Church. . . . No better citizen is there, whether in time of peace or war, than the Christian who is mindful of his duty; but such a one should be ready to suffer all things, even death itself, rather than abandon the cause of God or of the Church.[24]

The one positive right that is strongly defended by Leo is the right to private property. In what is perhaps his most famous encyclical, *Rerum Novarum*, presented May 15, 1891, the Roman pontiff argues that this right is absolutely fundamental in human societies:

> The common opinion of mankind, little affected by the few dissentients who have contended for the opposite view, has found in the careful study of nature, and in the laws of nature, the foundations of the division of property, and the practice of all ages has consecrated the principle of private ownership, as being preeminently in conformity with human nature, and as conducing in the most unmistakable manner to the peace and tranquility of human existence. The same principle is confirmed and enforced by the civil laws—laws which, so long as they are just, derive from the law of nature their binding force.[25]

Leo was convinced that all legitimate rights have their origin in nature. In order to understand any true right it is first necessary to understand the nature of man. A good illustration of this principle is Leo's explanation of how the right to own private property is linked very closely with the nature of the family:

> That right to property, therefore, which has been proved to belong naturally to individual persons, must in like wise belong to a man in his capacity of head of a family; nay, that right is all the stronger in proportion as the human person receives a wider extension in the family group. It is a most sacred law of nature that a father should provide food and all necessaries for those whom he has begotten; and, similarly, it is natural that he should wish that his children, who carry on, so to speak, and continue his personality, should be by him provided with all that is needful to enable them to keep themselves decently from want and misery amid the uncertainties of this mortal life. Now, in no other way can a father effect this except by the ownership of productive property, which he can transmit to his children by inheritance.[26]

When any given "right" is not based on the nature of man, it is not a true right for Leo. He was primarily concerned with the dignity of the human person rather than with a set of positive rights. This distinction is absolutely crucial for our understanding of Leo's thought. Even a scholar as careful and well-informed as Ernest L. Fortin may have misunderstood this all-important distinction. Fortin, in a fine analysis of *Rerum Novarum*, has argued that what Leo was trying to do in the encyclical was to make the "Lockean" doctrine of rights compatible with traditional Catholic social thought.[27] Obviously, I disagree with Fortin's reading of Leo's text. A close reading of *Rerum Novarum* along with *Libertas* shows that Leo's notion of rights was completely different from Locke's. For Leo, natural rights are based on the nature of man and on an immutable divine law. Locke's doctrine, which is neither theological nor ontological, stresses the freedom and the autonomy of the individual.

In Leo's day, women and children were routinely placed in factories to work like men. In *Rerum Novarum*, the Roman pontiff strongly condemned this practice. Leo was especially opposed to child labor:

Work which is quite suitable for a strong man cannot rightly be required from a woman or a child. And, in regard to children, great care should be taken not to place them in workshops and factories until their bodies and minds are sufficiently developed. For, just as very rough weather destroys the buds of spring, so does too early an experience of life's hard toil blight the young promise of a child's faculties, and render any true education impossible.[28]

These remarks may well have led some writers over the years to believe that Leo was a man of "liberal" or "modern" sensibilities, but, as we have seen, this view constitutes a misunderstanding of Leo's social teaching. Leo was interested most in the dignity of the human person. It is precisely for this reason that he wanted to protect women and children from "life's hard toil." This special interest in the plight of children is one of the features that distinguish Leo's thought from that of so many secular philosophers who came before him. The world, as Leo knew it, was not inhabited exclusively by men; his universe included men, women, and children. He also stressed the importance of the family, even going as far as to describe the "rights" of families:

> Provided, therefore, the limits which are prescribed by the very purposes for which it exists be not transgressed, the family has at least equal rights with the State in the choice and pursuit of the things needful to its preservation and its just liberty. We say, "at least equal rights"; for, inasmuch as the domestic household is antecedent, as well in idea as in fact, to the gathering of men into a community, the family must necessarily have rights and duties which are prior to those of the community, and founded more immediately in nature.[29]

Leo is very careful to state here that this notion remains true, provided that the purposes for which the family exists are not "transgressed." Obviously, he understood that the traditional notion of the family was under severe attack in his day. If we recall that socialism was attracting more and more followers during this period and that many writers were convinced that the family must be subsumed into the state, we understand the historical and social context of Leo's remarks.

Not many philosophers have defended the dignity of the human person and the family with as much passion as Leo XIII. In a sense, it is fortunate for Leo that he did not live to see how many of his grim predictions for the future would come true in the horrible century that was only in its infancy when he died at age ninety-three in 1903.

Chapter Six

THE SURVIVAL OF TRADITION

One of those teachers selected by Pope Leo "to implant the doctrine of Thomas Aquinas in the minds of students" was a Belgian priest named Desiré Joseph Mercier. Mercier was only twenty-eight years old when *Aeterni Patris* appeared in 1879, yet the encyclical seems to have left a lifelong impression on the young priest. Mercier, who had been ordained in 1874, would help to establish a chair in Thomistic philosophy at the University of Louvain.[1] A few years later, the Institut Supérieur de Philosophie was also founded at Louvain. In 1894, Mercier was named president of the Institut.[2] Clearly, Pope Leo's teachings had been received by the young Mercier and by others in Belgium with great enthusiasm.

Unlike many of the Thomists who had come before him, Mercier was very interested in modern science. He was especially interested in a newly emerging discipline, experimental psychology.[3] As a scholar he was strongly committed to the idea that all of the sciences could work together with philosophy to form a unified, rational whole.[4] Mercier's approach in this sense was much more open than that of most of his nineteenth-century predecessors. This fact, however, does not mean that Mercier necessarily embraced all modern philosophical ideas. He was, rather, quite skeptical of some modern philosophers, especially of the Germans, whom Mercier believed were responsible for the ethical deterioration of Germany:

> A mental atmosphere has been produced in Germany in which legal matters are divorced from moral right. Kant, Hegel, Nietzsche, have spread this through all ranks of society. In this

atmosphere, a militarist idea of things has been formed, and has gathered strength, according to which a nation has a right to live and to develop its life to any extent, without being answerable for its doings before that moral tribunal of the conscience which judges our every-day actions.[5]

Obviously, what Mercier could see in early-twentieth-century Germany was the rejection of the older natural-law tradition that, by that time, had been abandoned in most of Western Europe. He also understood the philosophical basis for this change better than most other observers. Indeed, by 1907, when he was named cardinal, Mercier had established an outstanding reputation as a scholar and was, without question, one of the leading Catholic intellectuals of his day.[6]

Cardinal Mercier, however, was much more than a keen observer of contemporary thought and events. What makes him different from so many other philosophers is that Mercier would have the opportunity to put his ideas into practice. Seven years after his appointment as cardinal, Belgium was occupied by German forces. His heroic stand against the Germans during the First World War made him an international celebrity. In many of Cardinal Mercier's letters and speeches we can see the strong influence of Thomas Aquinas. One quite explicit example of this doctrine is seen in an address entitled "For Our Soldiers," given on July 21, 1916, concerning justice and retribution:

> Whatever may be our sufferings, we must not wish to show hatred towards those who have inflicted them. Our national unity is joined with a feeling of universal brotherhood. But even this feeling of universal brotherhood is dominated by our respect for unconditional justice, without which no relationship is possible, either between individual or between nations.
>
> And that is why, with St. Thomas Aquinas, the most authoritative teacher of Christian Theology, we proclaim that public retribution is commendable.
>
> Crimes, violation of justice, outrage on the public peace, whether enacted by an individual or by a group, must be repressed. Men's minds are stirred up, tortured, uneasy, as long as the guilty one is not put back in his place, as the strong, healthy,

colloquial expression has it. To put men and things back in their places is to reestablish order, readjust the balance, and restore peace on a just basis.[7]

Cardinal Mercier's powerful sense of justice is clearly evident in this passage. His appeal here is not to any specific treaty or document of international agreement, but rather to a sense of natural justice, which is a fundamental part of natural law. In this insistence on natural justice rather than on any particular legal code we see that Mercier was quite similar in outlook to Pope Leo. Indeed, for both thinkers justice is the most fundamental issue in civil matters.

In a 1917 address to a group of clerics entitled, "Christian Vengeance," Mercier again refers specifically to the teachings of Thomas Aquinas. On this occasion, he offered a theological explanation for the justice of war:

The will to avenge an evil is properly a virtue. St. Thomas considers it as a special virtue which completes in each of us our natural repulsion for everything hurtful to us, makes us repel an injury which menaces us, and incites us to take vengeance for it after we have received it. What would you say of a man who, under the pretext of kindness, would endeavor to close all prisons and suppress the penal code?

The collective crime of a nation which violates the rights of another nation is incomparably more grave than the crime of an individual whom society sends to the guillotine or the scaffold. We well understand that those who doubt the justice of their cause seek to see in war only subjects for pity or horror. But for us war is the means of making honor respected and right triumph, and of reestablishing on a pinnacle truth and the worship of the God who is Truth. Herein lies the grandeur and nobility of war and the justification of all its sacrifices.[8]

On the basis of Thomistic principles, Mercier has provided an argument for a just war against the Germans. More specifically, what the cardinal does in this passage is to start from a discussion of personal virtue and extend his argument to society as a whole. His position is that natural justice requires personal defense. When we apply the same principle to entire nations, it is clear that nations must also defend themselves. Otherwise, neither truth nor justice is served. Ultimately, God, who is truth itself, is not served when injustice is allowed to prevail. Mercier thus provides a justification for the Belgian war effort which is both natural and theological.

Neither Leo XIII nor Mercier defended moral or ethical principles compatible with modern secular liberalism. Both men were strict Thomists; as such, both embraced a doctrine of absolute and immutable truth. When Mercier challenged the practice of the German occupation forces of deporting young men from Belgium so that these same men could work in German factories, thus contributing to the war effort of the enemy, he was well aware of existing international treaties that condemned this action; however, his denunciation of this practice was based on the principles of traditional natural law rather than modern international law. When Pope Leo defended the "rights" of workers in *Rerum Novarum*, his arguments were not based on liberal principles; Leo's defense, like Mercier's, was based on natural right and justice. At the beginning of the twentieth century, this natural-law tradition was still alive in Western Europe, but its days were numbered; the liberal doctrine that had been spawned by early modern philosophy and nurtured by British empiricism and French rationalism, would soon eclipse the older tradition.

The first two decades of the twentieth century formed a young Frenchman destined to become one of the century's giants of Catholic thought. Jacques Maritain was born in Paris in 1882, only three years after *Aeterni Patris* had appeared. After studying biology at the Sorbonne, he and Raissa Oumansoff, the woman who would soon become his bride, attended the lectures of Henry Bergson at the Collège de France.[9] Bergson's thought had a profound impact on the young couple. Jacques and Raissa had been looking desperately for someone who could provide some direction in an intellectual world that had no sense of the absolute. Bergson was the man who helped the couple find that direction. In 1906, under the influence of the writer Leon Bloy, Jacques and Raissa became converts to Roman Catholicism.[10] A short time afterward, Jacques began to study the works of Thomas Aquinas.

So great was his passion for this subject that Maritain would later be recognized as one of the great Thomists of the entire century.[11]

Although Maritain would not enter religious life until near the end of his life (after Raissa's death), he had much in common with Cardinal Mercier. Both men were Thomists with advanced training in modern scientific disciplines. As philosophers, both men also firmly believed that Thomistic principles could inform modern scientific knowledge. Maritain and Mercier were more interested in transforming modern thought than in merely rejecting it. However, if there are similarities, there are also notable differences between the two men. Maritain's early years were spent looking for truth outside the Church. He was exposed much more to secular writers and artists than to scholastic or Christian philosophers. Maritain's intellectual circle during this period has been described in some detail by Yves Simon:

> I have some notion of the people whose company he liked, for, over a long period, it was my privilege to visit his home on Sunday afternoons. The living room was generally crowded, less by teachers or students than by writers, poets, painters, musicians, persons interested in mysticism, missionaries and friends of the missions. Most of the artists were of the vanguard description. Concerning Maritain's philosophical education, the important fact is that he studied under Bergson.[12]

This association with secular thinkers left a permanent impression on the young Maritain. One of the reasons why he was such an eclectic thinker may well have been this early experience. It is certainly true that Maritain was not limited by an education that taught him to approach intellectual matters in a traditional or conventional way. Indeed, if it is true that Maritain can be described accurately as the man who later would defend the Church and traditional Christian philosophy against modern secularism, it must be noted that he accomplished this task as a man of the world.

During the early decades of the twentieth century, the old Catholic tradition was still alive in France. Thus authors such as Maritain, Leon Bloy (1846–1917), Paul Claudel (1868–1955), George Bernanos (1888–1948), and François Mauriac (1885–1970) were not considered merely *French* writers, but rather French *Catholic* writers. Even within this group, Maritain had strong disagreements. Perhaps one of the best examples of these differences of opinion can be seen in Maritain's position on the Spanish Civil War. During that conflict, Maritain refused to pledge his unconditional support for the Nationalists. This action was strongly criticized by many Catholic authors, including Paul Claudel.[13] Maritain's position, however, was not anti-Catholic; it was antifascist and anti-Franco. He understood that the Nationalists had committed a number of atrocities during the war and refused to ignore this fact. He also believed that the massacre of the poor was just as wrong and sinful as the murder of priests, remarking, "it is a horrible sacrilege to massacre priests, even if they are 'fascist' (they are the ministers of Christ), out of hatred for religion; and it is another sacrilege, just as horrible, to massacre the poor, even though they are 'marxists' (they are the people of Christ), in the name of religion."[14] Maritain was a man of principle; he was opposed to the cruelty of both sides in this conflict. His courageous stand on this issue later won for him the support of some Catholic writers, including Mauriac.[15]

Maritain, a man of deep faith and intense piety, was a great admirer of Leo XIII; he knew Leo's encyclicals quite well and was quite familiar with his social teachings. However, Maritain was different in outlook from the Roman pontiff. Indeed, if Leo only reluctantly accepted democracy, Maritain was absolutely convinced that democracy was the most attractive form of government. Maritain also believed that in the ideal political society, which for him would take the form of a Christian democracy, the Church would cooperate with a democratic state to defend the fundamental principles of human dignity:

> Just as democracy must, under penalty of disintegration, foster and defend the democratic charter; so a Christian democracy, that is, a democracy fully aware of its own sources, must, under penalty of disintegration, keep alive in itself the Christian sense of human dignity and human equality, of justice and freedom.[16]

Maritain was perhaps one of the strongest Catholic defenders of democracy in his day. He was convinced that this form of government was best suited to protect the dignity of the human person. One of the reasons that Maritain believed this was that a democratic form of government, based on a principle of pluralism, could protect the rights of many different groups within the same state. Maritain, who lived in America almost twenty years, was also a great admirer of the American Constitution, which he considered a fine example of a Christian constitution:

> Far beyond the influences received either from Locke or the XVIIIth Century Enlightenment, the Constitution of this country is deep-rooted in the age-old heritage of Christian thought and civilization. . . . Peerless is the significance, for political philosophy, of the establishment of the American Constitution at the end of the XVIIIth Century. This Constitution can be described as an outstanding lay Christian document tinged with the philosophy of the day.[17]

Not only did Maritain admire the Constitution, he was very impressed with the way religion could be observed in so many aspects of American public life:

> The spirit and inspiration of this great political Christian document is basically repugnant to the idea of making human society stand aloof from God and from any religious faith. Thanksgiving and public prayer, the invocation of the name of God at the occasion of any major official gathering, are, in the practical behaviour of the nation, a token of this very same spirit and inspiration.[18]

Maritain, who died in 1973, saw only the beginning of the secular changes that have taken place in American society since the publication of these ideas in his book, *Man and the State*, over fifty years ago. One can only imagine what he would have thought if he had witnessed the ongoing and constant legal battles to keep prayer and religion out of every facet of American public life today.

Although Maritain was committed to the principles of modern democracy, in philosophical outlook, he was a traditionalist. In fact, as we noted earlier, he embraced Thomism as few philosophers have since his day. As a Thomist, Maritain was also a strong defender of natural law. In *Man and the State* Maritain offers a short but precise summary of the history of this doctrine:

The genuine idea of natural law is a heritage of Greek and Christian thought. It goes back not only to Grotius, who indeed began deforming it, but, before him to Suarez and Francisco de Vitoria; and further back to St. Thomas Aquinas . . . and still further back to St. Augustine and the Church Fathers and St. Paul (we remember St. Paul's saying: "When the Gentiles who have not the Law, do by nature the things contained in the Law, these, having not the Law, are a law unto themselves . . . "); and even further back to Cicero, to the Stoics, to the great moralists of antiquity and its great poets, particularly Sophocles. Antigone, who was aware that in transgressing the human law and being crushed by it she was obeying a better commandment, the unwritten and unchangeable laws, is the eternal heroine of natural law.[19]

Obviously, Maritain belonged to the traditional school of natural law. His doctrine was, therefore, shaped by ancient and medieval philosophy. Maritain was convinced that the philosophical principles that had formed the more modern doctrine of human rights (that is, Kantian autonomy and absolute freedom) had separated man from God. He was also quite certain that this doctrine, based on these same principles, was destined to fail. For Maritain, this problem had already led many people to question and even reject the whole notion of human rights:

This philosophy built no solid foundations for the rights of the human person, because nothing can be founded on illusion: it compromised and squandered these rights, because it led men to conceive them as rights in themselves divine, hence infinite, escaping every objective measure, denying every limitation imposed upon the claims of the ego, and ultimately expressing the absolute independence of the human subject and a so-called absolute right—which supposedly pertains to everything in the human subject by the mere fact that it is in him—to unfold one's cherished possibilities at the expense of all other beings. When men thus instructed clashed on all sides with the impossible, they came to believe in the bankruptcy of the rights of the human person. Some have turned against these rights with an enslaver's fury; some have continued to invoke them, while in their inmost conscience they are weighed down by a temptation to scepticism which is one of the most alarming symptoms of the crisis of our civilization.[20]

Maritain could see that without a solid philosophical foundation and an "objective measure" it was only a matter of time before the modern notion of human rights would lose all credence. He was well aware of the fact that many of those who invoke a rights doctrine are often quite skeptical of any deeper or more enduring meaning. Often, the substance of the doctrine is no longer understood by the very people who would defend it. The modern notion of human rights has become a doctrine of entitlement and victim protection. The dignity of the human person has little to do with this modern aberration.

For Maritain, natural law is ontological; therefore, it reflects the natural order of being. As such, natural law expresses an obligation that human beings have *by nature*. If there is no ontological foundation for human rights, these rights must be based exclusively on reason:

> I have said that natural law is unwritten law; it is unwritten law in the deepest sense of that expression, because our knowledge of it is no work of free conceptualization, but results from a conceptualization bound to the essential inclination of being, of living nature, and of reason which are at work in man, and because it develops in proportion to the degree of moral experience and self-reflection, and of social experience also, of which man is capable in the various ages of his history. Thus it is that in ancient and mediaeval times attention was paid, in natural law, to the obligations of man more than to his rights.[21]

Maritain here stresses the difference between rights and obligations. Indeed, in the older natural law tradition, obligation is far more important than personal rights. Maritain makes it clear that the modern doctrine of "the rights of man" is a product of the Enlightenment. What Maritain most wanted was to reconcile these two traditions within the context of natural law, thus establishing a firmer foundation for the modern doctrine of human rights.

Without question, Maritain's thought has had a powerful influence on Catholic intellectuals for several decades. The attempt to reconcile traditional natural law with the modern doctrine of human rights was certainly one of the most important issues for the Second Vatican Council (1962–65). One of the key documents on this question is the papal encyclical, *Pacem in Terris*, presented by John XXIII on April 11, 1963. In the encyclical, Pope John describes a whole series of natural rights, including rights related to religious, economic, personal and political life, all of which are understood within the context of the dignity of the human person:

> Any well-regulated and productive association of men in society demands the acceptance of one fundamental principle: that each individual man is truly a person. He has a nature, that is endowed with intelligence and free will. As such he has rights and duties, which together flow as a direct consequence from his nature. These rights and duties are universal and inviolable, and therefore altogether inalienable. When, furthermore, we consider man's personal dignity from the standpoint of divine revelation, inevitably our estimate of it is incomparably increased.[22]

If indeed Pope John's extensive treatment of human rights does not represent a departure from previous Catholic thought, the notion of natural rights is certainly greatly expanded. For Pope John, natural rights extend far beyond freedom of worship and material well-being; he defends the right to free expression (within the limits of the common good) and education, even defending the right to higher education for those in society who are talented and who might then contribute to society:

> He has a right to freedom in investigating the truth, and—within the limits of the moral order and the common good—to freedom of speech and publication, and the freedom to pursue whatever profession he may choose. He has the right, also, to be accurately informed about public events. He has the natural right to share in the benefits of culture, and hence to receive a good general education, and a technical or professional training consistent with the degree of educational development in his

own country. Furthermore, a system must be devised for affording gifted members of society the opportunity of engaging in more advanced studies, with a view to their occupying, as far as possible, positions of responsibility in society in keeping with their natural talent and acquired skill.[23]

One of the reasons that Pope John's doctrine of natural rights is more extensive than that found in earlier papal encyclicals is that he has taken the notion of the dignity of the human person to a new level. For Pope John, not only does a human being have the right to be protected from social evils; each individual human being should have the right to flourish in society based on his or her natural talents. This is a new idea and one that distinguishes Pope John's thought from that of previous popes. Pope John, however, is careful not to break completely with the older tradition. At one point in *Pacem in Terris*, when the Roman pontiff discusses social order, he returns to the teaching of Thomas Aquinas:

> Now the order which prevails in human society is wholly incorporeal in nature. Its foundation is truth, and it must be brought into effect by justice. It needs to be animated and perfected by men's love for one another, and, while preserving freedom intact, it must make for an equilibrium in society which is increasingly more human in character. But such an order—universal, absolute and immutable in its principles—finds its source in the true, personal and transcendent God. He is the first truth, the sovereign good, and as such the deepest source from which human society, if it is to be properly constituted, creative, and worthy of man's dignity, draws its genuine vitality. This is what St. Thomas means when he says: "Human reason is the standard which measures the degree of goodness of the human will, and as such it derives from the eternal law, which is divine reason. . . . Hence it is clear that the goodness of the human will depends much more on the eternal law than on human reason."[24]

This reference to the Thomistic doctrine is extremely important. It is only within the context of eternal law that "universal," "absolute," or "immutable" principles can be established. Pope John may not have been, like his predecessor, Leo XIII, a strict Thomist, but he did understand Thomas's importance for Catholic thought. If the Thomistic influence is somewhat more limited in the social thought of Pope John, the notion of the dignity of the human person is not. Indeed, on the basis of this principle, Pope John took the rights doctrine found in *Rerum Novarum* and expanded it to establish a newer, more comprehensive set of human rights.

The principles developed in *Pacem in Terris* have had a powerful influence on Catholic social thought since its appearance in 1963. Thomistic philosophy and theology however, have not been so fortunate. After the Second Vatican Council, many new schools of theology have appeared as the overall influence of Thomism has declined.[25] Many Catholic theologians have now completely rejected Thomism. Despite this tendency, however, traditional natural law has not disappeared from official Church teaching. The Roman pontiff, John Paul II, may well have been the strongest defender of natural law since the time of Leo XIII. Although one can find many references to this doctrine in his teachings, one of the pope's most comprehensive statements on this question appeared in the 1993 encyclical *Veritatis Splendor*:

> The moral law has its origin in God and always finds its source in him: at the same time, by virtue of natural reason, which derives from divine wisdom, it is a properly human law. Indeed, as we have seen, the natural law "is nothing other than the light of understanding infused in us by God, whereby we understand what must be done and what must be avoided. God gave this law to man at creation." The rightful autonomy of the practical reason means that man possesses in himself his own law, received from the Creator. Nevertheless, the autonomy of reason can not mean that reason itself creates values and moral norms.[26]

In this passage, Pope John Paul establishes two absolutely fundamental points. The first of these is that natural law is derived from God. The text utilized by the pope (in quotation marks) to prove his argument is taken directly from the works of Thomas.[27] The second point established here by John Paul is that there does, indeed, exist an autonomous human law; however, this "rightful autonomy" is "received from the Creator"; it cannot be created by an independent human reason. Clearly, a moral system based on a notion like Kantian autonomy was totally unacceptable for the Roman pontiff.

John Paul understood that for many modern scholars the first principle that must be accepted is that of absolute freedom. For these same writers, the idea that nature itself directs moral reason is untenable. However, according to the pope, this modern view has serious moral consequences, because, ultimately, it divides the human person and reduces the human body to mere matter:

> A freedom which claims to be absolute ends up treating the human body as a raw datum, devoid of any meaning and moral values until freedom has shaped it in accordance with its design. Consequently, human nature and the body appear as presuppositions or preambles, materially necessary, for freedom to make its choice, yet extrinsic to the person, the subject and the human act. Their functions would not be able to constitute reference points for moral decisions, because the finalities of these inclinations would be merely "physical" goods, called by some premoral. To refer to them, in order to find in them rational indications with regard to the order of morality, would be to expose oneself to the accusations of physicalism or biologism. In this way of thinking, the tension between freedom and a nature conceived of in a reductive way is resolved by a division within man himself.[28]

The argument that nature is morally neutral (which makes all appeal to a natural end meaningless) is absolutely fundamental for those who claim that the notion of natural law is groundless. These same writers argue that "human nature" is a purely human construction.

One of the features that made natural law so attractive for the Roman pontiff was its universality. In contemporary thought, however, almost any doctrine that claims a universal application is looked upon with suspicion. It is for this very reason that natural law is taken far less seriously than the powerful influence of culture. When culture is considered more fundamental than philosophical principle, values become relative (changing with different groups over time). Ultimately, individual human beings become independent agents who choose what is best for themselves. The individual then becomes far more important than any general principle of morality. Pope John Paul was well aware of this difficulty; his argument, however, was that it is precisely natural law that brings to light the dignity of the human person:

> The separation which some have posited between the freedom of individuals and the nature which all have in common, as it emerges from certain philosophical theories which are highly influential in present-day culture, obscures the perception of the universality of the moral law on the part of reason. But inasmuch as the natural law expresses the dignity of the human person and lays the foundation for his fundamental rights and duties, it is universal in its precepts and its authority extends to all mankind. This universality does not ignore the individuality of human beings, nor is it opposed to the absolute uniqueness of each person. On the contrary, it embraces at its root each of the person's free acts, which are meant to bear witness to the universality of the true good.[29]

This notion of the dignity and uniqueness of the human person may well have been the most important social teaching of the Roman pontiff. We find many references to this doctrine in his encyclicals. In this sense, the pope's thought shows the influence of the ideas expressed in *Pacem in Terris*.

Pope John Paul shared a profound respect for the dignity of the human person with John XXIII. He also inherited a powerful sense of social justice from Pope Leo. In *Centesimus Annus*, a 1991 encyclical commemorating the hundredth anniversary of Leo's *Rerum Novarum*, Pope John Paul addressed the social and economic problems of the late twentieth century utilizing the same moral and philosophical principles as those used by Leo a hundred years before.[30] Like Leo, John Paul stressed the importance of understanding freedom within the context of truth. Without this primary concern for truth, the notion of freedom is groundless. The Roman pontiff informed us that the notion of "rights" is also meaningless without a foundation in truth, reminding us of Leo's warning in *Rerum Novarum* concerning the separation of truth and rights:

> Reading the encyclical within the context of Pope Leo's whole magisterium, we see how it points essentially to the socioeconomic consequences of an error which has even greater implications. As has been mentioned, this error consists in an understanding of human freedom which detaches it from obedience to the truth and consequently from the duty to respect the rights of others. The essence of freedom then becomes self-love which leads to the point of contempt for God and neighbor, a self-love which refuses to be limited by any demand of justice.[31]

The horrible results of this self-love are then shown in graphic terms by Pope John Paul, who presented the brutal history of the first half of the twentieth century, insisting that this series of tragedies was best explained as the consequence of the modern contempt for God and neighbor:

> This very error had extreme consequences in the tragic series of wars which ravaged Europe and the world between 1914 and 1945. Some of these resulted from militarism and exaggerated nationalism, and from related forms of totalitarianism; some derived from the class struggle; still others were civil wars or wars of an ideological nature. Without the terrible burden of hatred and resentment which had built up as a result of so many injustices both on the international level and within individual states, such cruel wars would not have been possible in which great nations invested their energies and in which there was no hesitation to violate the most sacred human rights, with the extermination of entire peoples and social groups being planned and carried out. Here we recall the Jewish people in particular, whose terrible fate has become a symbol of the aberration of which man is capable when he turns against God.[32]

For the Roman pontiff, humanity is doomed when it turns away from God. The hundred years of tragedy that we have experienced since the time of Pope Leo are a testimony to the truth of this sobering observation. Nevertheless, few people today accept the claim that nature can direct reason in its search for moral principles. Most are skeptical of any notion of absolute truth and fewer still are interested in obedience to God. John Paul's world was far more secular than Leo's, yet the Roman pontiff accepted the same philosophical and moral principles that his predecessor had defended so adamantly a century before. This is so because John Paul believed, like Leo, that truth is immutable and that only what is true can endure.

In *Fides et Ratio*, an encyclical letter delivered on September 14, 1998, the Roman pontiff explained how modern thought had abandoned the search for truth in favor of an investigation of "human subjectivity" and "experimental data":

> Complex systems of thought have thus been built, yielding results in the different fields of knowledge and fostering the development of culture and history. Anthropology, logic, the natural sciences, history, linguistics and so forth—the whole universe of knowledge has been involved in one way or another. Yet the positive results achieved must not obscure the fact that reason, in its one-sided concern to investigate human subjectivity, seems to have forgotten that men and women are always called to direct their steps toward a truth which transcends them. Sundered from that truth, individuals are at the mercy of caprice, and their state as person ends up being judged by pragmatic criteria based essentially upon experimental data in the mistaken belief that technology must dominate all.[33]

Clearly, the Roman pontiff was deeply troubled by the fact that the status of the individual as person had become less important for the advocates of experimental and "pragmatic" science. When science takes this turn human beings fall prey to technology and "are at the mercy of caprice." In particular, Pope John Paul observed that modern thought was no longer concerned primarily with the "truth of being," that is to say, an ontological understanding of truth:

> It has happened therefore that reason, rather than voicing the human orientation toward truth, has wilted under the weight of

so much knowledge and little by little has lost the capacity to lift its gaze to the heights, not daring to rise to the truth of being. Abandoning the investigation of being, modern philosophical research has concentrated instead upon human knowing. Rather than make use of the human capacity to know the truth, modern philosophy has preferred to accentuate the ways in which this capacity is limited and conditioned.[34]

For Pope John Paul, the importance of this ontological understanding of truth could not be overestimated. The investigation of "being" must provide the foundation for a philosophical system that supports an immutable moral order. Without this stable foundation morality would be relegated (at best) to a series of arbitrary dictates of reason or "categorical imperatives" that reasonable people accept out of a sense of duty. Without a grounding in being, morality itself must evolve as the new discoveries of the social and biological sciences shape a new consciousness. Indeed, the Roman pontiff was absolutely convinced that without the objectivity provided by this philosophy of being, human freedom and dignity could not survive:

> It should never be forgotten that the neglect of being inevitably leads to losing touch with objective truth and therefore with the very ground of human dignity. This in turn makes it possible to erase from the countenance of man and woman the marks of their likeness to God, and thus to lead them little by little either to a destructive will to power or to a solitude without hope. Once the truth is denied to human beings, it is pure illusion to try to set them free. Truth and freedom either go together hand in hand or together they perish in misery.[35]

Pope John Paul was absolutely committed to the notion that moral systems without this foundation in being can claim no lasting or enduring validity, since he believed that only an ontological morality could support a permanent natural law. Without the "objective truth" which being provides "truth is denied to human beings." The skepticism that so characterizes our time (as Maritain observed) was completely absent from the teachings of John Paul.

In recent years, some writers have tried to revive natural law, but, generally speaking, these efforts have been attempts to introduce a modified version of the doctrine. In 1977, Michael Crowe's study *The Changing Profile of the Natural Law* appeared. This book provides a solid history of the natural-law tradition up to the time of Vatican II. In the last chapter of his text, Crowe proposed some suggestions so that natural law (which Crowe believed was no longer viable in its traditional form) could be salvaged. In some instances, these views reflect the very positions later criticized by Pope John Paul in *Fides et Ratio*:

> The auxiliary studies of anthropology and sociology help us to avoid the trap of an over-hasty identification of precepts as timeless and unchanging when, in fact, they are time-conditioned and culture-bound. One would be far more circumspect today than in the past in asserting, for instance, that private property is a matter of the natural law, or that to take interest on money is unnatural or that woman comes under the natural dominion of man.[36]

Crowe, whose ideas show the powerful influence of modern social sciences, was convinced that notions like that of an "immutable" truth or a "timeless" morality are simply illusions. For Crowe, the more precise way of understanding moral precepts is to consider them "time-conditioned and culture-bound." When Crowe's book was written, no one knew that John Paul II would write *Veritatis Splendor*, *Centessimus Annus*, and *Fides et Ratio*. All of these texts address moral questions in terms of traditional natural law. In effect, the doctrine that Crowe thought could not survive has flourished in key papal encyclicals since 1977.

Without question, one of the most important studies of Thomas's legal and political thought to appear in recent years is John Finnis's book *Aquinas: Moral, Political, and Legal Theory*.[37] Finnis, one of the most distinguished natural-law theorists working today, is a great admirer of the philosophy of Thomas Aquinas. His study may be described accurately as an attempt to both elucidate and defend the reasonableness of the Thomistic system. As we saw in chapter 2, Finnis stresses the importance of human rights in Thomas's thought. In fact, for Finnis, these rights are absolutely fundamental:

Although Aquinas' main discussion of right(s) is in the context of justice considered as a virtue—as an aspect of good character—he takes care to exclude these suppositions. For he makes it clear that justice's primary demand is that the relevant "external acts" be done; they need not be done out of respect for justice, or as a manifestation or result of good character. So: the good of justice [*bonum iustitiae*] is not the "clean hands" (better: clean heart) of those who are to do justice but rather—what Aquinas puts at the head of his treatise on justice—justice's very object: the right(s) of the human person entitled to the equal treatment we call justice. Aquinas' morality and politics is a matter of rights just as fundamentally as it is a matter of duties and of excellences of individual and communal character.[38]

This reading makes Aquinas a defender of "equal treatment" and therefore, of equal rights. In effect, what Finnis has done with this argument is to make Thomas a modern thinker. The natural order of justice, which in Aquinas's thought is based on the natural order of being, is completely absent from this description. In fact, Finnis is even willing to argue that external acts "need not be done out of respect for justice." Obviously, what Finnis has done is to limit the sense of justice to that of personal virtue in this section of his book on the importance of rights. If, indeed, rights are to have any meaning at all, they must be understood within a larger context of "general justice." Earlier in his study Finnis provides a very good description of this notion: "The basis for this all-embracing justice is, once again, the fact that the human good(s) to which practical reason directs us are good(s) for human beings as such, and so for every human being."[39] Any external action that would violate this justice would be absolutely wrong. When we talk about basic "good(s) for human beings as such" the issue becomes one of nature and being. Ultimately, justice must be connected to ontological theology in Thomas's system. Alasdair MacIntyre explains this point quite clearly:

> What, then, is the peculiar place of justice within this scheme? The right place to begin is not with Aquinas' discussions of the virtues, but with his metaphysical theology. For just as there is an

inescapably theological dimension to prudence even as a natural virtue, so there is also such a dimension to justice . . . that there is such a timeless standard of justice is a claim ultimately grounded on a theological understanding of the ordering of things.[40]

Thomas does not limit the scope of justice in the *Prima secundae* to make morality more practical and less theoretical. His system functions as a whole, not with different limitations assigned to his terms in the different parts. The principles of the *Prima pars* must also apply to the remaining sections of the *Summa*. Justice cannot be restricted to the realm of personal virtue: it must have a much broader application within the context of an ontological theology.

Although Finnis avoids ontological considerations in his treatment of rights theory in Aquinas, he does at least mention "being" in other sections of his book. We find one very good example in his examination of marriage and sexuality:

> The well-being of children, and so of the whole set of human communities, depends on the unreserved, long-term commitment of pairs of persons fitted by their biological, emotional, dispositional complementarity—as persons of opposite sex—to be parents (which includes the generation, gestation, nurture, education, and care of "this child, these children, of ours"). But this commitment needs to be expressed, experienced, and actualized in the marital intercourse which unites the two spouses at all levels of their being.[41]

Finnis clearly understands that this consideration of being is of major importance in our understanding of morality. However, for Finnis acts which are contrary to the natural order of being are wrong first of all because they are contrary to reason and only secondarily because they are contrary to nature. Finnis makes this very point when he discusses the moral unacceptability of extramarital sex. Finnis states that "extra-marital sex [*luxuria*] both is contrary to the good of marriage and offends against love-of-neighbour, and for both reasons is against reason, and consequently against nature."[42] Finnis is convinced that reason comes first in Aquinas's thinking. That is to say, actions are to be considered right or wrong first of all because they are in accord with reason and *then* because they conform to the natural order of being. This point is of primary importance for Finnis; ultimately, for him, natural law in Aquinas must be understood as an appeal to the mind:

> Aquinas strongly insists that law is something addressed by one mind and will to others—by one freely choosing person to other freely choosing persons. This does not contradict the idea of an eternal law governing even subrational creatures, but it firmly relegates that idea to an extended, non-focal sense of "law." The central case of law is an appeal to the mind, the choice, the moral strength [virtus], and the love of those subject to the law.[43]

Eternal law must be considered secondary in this reading. What matters most is not the natural order of being but rather the mind and will of "freely choosing persons" who, on the bases of "moral strength" and "love," choose to obey a law freely ordained by God. It is for this very reason that the notion of "practical reasonableness" is the most important for Finnis in his reading of Aquinas's moral philosophy. In the last chapter of his study, Finnis describes the application of this doctrine in theological terms that transform it into a form of participation in the mind of God:

> Practical reasonableness itself can also be seen now in a new light. It has a *further overarching point*, which subsumes, embraces, confirms, and explains all the other reasons for action, and which like all practical reasons is both individual and common, a reason both for individual and for interpersonal, group choices and actions. This further, more ultimate point [*finis*] is: to be as *like* God as human persons can be. For that is how we can participate well in—and give our own life the characteristics of—that activity which not only is supremely intelligent, free, self-possessed, and generous, but also must make best sense of everything.[44]

This "overarching" application makes the doctrine the most fundamental for moral human beings. Indeed, for Finnis, it is precisely this notion of practical reasonableness which "subsumes, embraces, confirms, and explains all the other reasons for action." In the end, it is this very notion that makes the "best sense of everything." The problem with this doctrine is that it presupposes a movement from the mind of a free human being directly to the mind of God. While it is true that this explanation allows Finnis to avoid the charge of ascribing to Aquinas a doctrine of moral autonomy, it nevertheless removes from the process an ontological ordering of things. Finnis is absolutely right to stress the importance of God's will in Aquinas's thought, but when the importance of man's natural end is left out of the equation, we are left with a doctrine that begins with human freedom and ends with man's participation in the divine mind with no consideration of man's nature.

Most of the essential features of Finnis's treatment of practical reasonableness in Aquinas were developed almost forty years ago in a brilliant essay published by Germain Grisez.[45] In that now classic study, Grisez directly addressed the question of whether or not "good" as a term convertible with "being" should be considered a part of practical reason:

> Some interpreters mistakenly ask whether the word "good" in the first principle has a transcendental or an ethical sense. The issue is a false one, for there is no question of extending the meaning of "good" to the amplitude of the transcendentals convertible with "being." The very text clearly indicates that Aquinas is concerned with good as the object of practical reason; hence the goods signified by the "good" of the first principle will be *human* goods. It must be so, since the good pursued by practical reason is an objective of *human* action.[46]

Once again, with this limitation placed on the notion of "good" in human action the connection with being is necessarily absent from our consideration. Even though Grisez and Finnis succeed in providing a logically consistent interpretation of this section of the *Summa*, they have achieved this consistency by distorting the true meaning of Thomas's text. This is so because on a more fundamental level good and being are actually the same in Aquinas's thought. Thomas explains this point very clearly early in the *Summa*:

> Good and being are really the same, and differ only according to reason, which is clear from the following argument. The essence

of good consists in this, that it is in some way desirable. Hence the Philosopher says "The good is what all desire." Now it is clear that a thing is desirable only in so far as it is perfect; for all desire their own perfection. But everything is perfect in so far as it is in act. Therefore it is clear that a thing is good so far as it is being; for it is being that is the actuality of all things, as is clear from the foregoing.[47]

We see in this text that for Thomas being and good in the most fundamental sense cannot be separated: what is good is what has achieved actuality in being. In terms of human action, the good corresponds to what is perfect or complete. Actions which make human beings true and complete human beings are good.[48] In traditional natural law, nature functions like being in this context. That is to say, those actions which are in accord with nature are good, while those that run counter to nature are evil. Grisez is critical of Suárez for defending this very position:

Suarez thinks that what is morally good or bad depends simply upon the agreement or disagreement of action with nature, and he holds that the obligation to do the one and to avoid the other arises from the imposition of the will of God. Hence "evil" in the first principle of natural law denotes only the actions which definitely disagree with nature, the doing of which is forbidden, and "good" denotes only the actions whose omission definitely disagrees with nature, the doing of which is commanded.[49]

While it is true that the philosophical positions of Suárez are not always exactly the same as those of Aquinas, the doctrine with which Grisez finds fault here is standard in traditional natural-law doctrine. Grisez objects to the notion that the morally good or bad is grounded in nature. Both Aquinas and Suárez are strongly committed to the principle that morality is grounded in nature. Virtually all of the defenders of traditional natural law understand the morally good in this manner.

Grisez is quite explicit about his position on the relationship between nature and practical reason:

If the first principle of practical reason restricted human good to the goods proportionate to nature, then a supernatural end for human action would be excluded. The relation of man to such an end could be established only by a leap into the transrational where human action would be impossible and where faith would replace natural law rather than supplement it.[50]

Aquinas has a distinctly different view on this question. For Thomas, nature does not preclude a supernatural end for human beings. On the contrary, man is led to God by his very nature. This is so because man is a being created by God in his image. As such, man naturally desires his ultimate end. Therefore, man by his nature desires to be like God. This urge does not require "a leap into the transrational"; it is, rather, an essential part of man's being:

> Besides, it is quite evident that things "naturally desire to be," and if they can be corrupted by anything they naturally resist corrupting agents and tend toward a place where they may be preserved, as fire inclines upward and earth downward. Now, all things get their being from the fact that they are made like unto God, Who is subsisting being itself, for all things exist merely as participants in existing being. Therefore, all things desire as their ultimate end to be made like unto God.
>
> Moreover, all created things are, in a sense, images of the first agent, that is, God, "for the agent makes a product to his own likeness." Now, the function of a perfect image is to represent its prototype by likeness to it; this is why an image is made. Therefore, all things exist in order to attain to the divine likeness, as to their ultimate end.[51]

In the Thomistic system, this ontological dimension is absolutely fundamental. Man must always be understood in relation to God. The relationship between man and God is not merely that of a creator and creature; it is of an ontological nature, where man (the created rational substance) as a being participates in divine being. This aspect of the human person informs all of the other aspects.

The doctrine that Finnis and Grisez find in Aquinas's thought may, indeed, be called "natural law," but it certainly is not the traditional version that we have described in this study. That form cannot be understood apart from considerations of nature and being.[52] In the early twenty-first century, very few thinkers still embrace traditional natural law. Nevertheless, as we have shown, this doctrine has survived in an intellectual world that has rejected almost any notion of ontological reality and understands the human person and morality in purely biological and cultural terms. For most modern thinkers, traditional natural law is like a face that no one can bear to look upon anymore. Indeed, it is a face disfigured by time and neglect.

Notes

Introduction

1. *In Plurimis*, text taken from *The Papal Encyclicals, 1878–1903*, ed. Claudia Carlen Ihm (Ann Arbor: Pierian Press, 1981), 2:159–167.

2. Ibid., 160.

3. Cicero, *De Legibus*, ed. and trans. Clinton Walker Keyes (Cambridge, Mass.: Harvard University Press, 1977), 347.

4. The Latin text reads, "Praecepta legis naturae hoc modo se habent ad rationem practicam sicut principia prima demonstrationum se habent ad rationem speculativam: utraque enim sunt quaedam principia per se nota." St. Thomas Aquinas, *Summa Theologiae* 1–2, q. 94, art. 2 (New York: Blackfriars, 1964) 28:78–79. For an excellent discussion of this text, see Ralph McInerny, *Aquinas on Human Action* (Washington, D.C.: Catholic University of America Press, 1992), 113–122.

5. The text is from book 5, lecture 12: "Sicut enim in speculativis sunt quaedam naturaliter cognita, ut principia indemonstrabilia et quae sunt propinqua his; quaedam vero studio hominum adinventa, et quae sunt propinqua; ita etiam in operativis sunt quaedam principia naturaliter cognita quasi indemonstrabilia principia et propinqua his, ut malum esse vitandum, nulli esse iniuste nocendum, non furandum, et similia. Alia vero sunt per industriam hominum excogitata, quae dicuntur hic iusta legalia." From *In decem libros Ethicorum Aristotelis ad Nicomachum expositio*, ed. Raymundi M. Spiazzi, OP (Rome: Marietti, 1964), 280. The English translation is from St. Thomas Aquinas, *Commentary on Aristotle's Nicomachean Ethics*, trans. C. I. Litzinger, OP (Notre Dame, Ind.: Dumb Ox Books, 1993), 325.

6. "Sed cum iustum naturale sit semper et ubique, ut dictum est, hoc non competit iusto legali vel positivo. Et ideo necesse est quod quicquid ex iusto naturali sequitur, quasi conclusio, sit iustum naturale; sicut ex hoc quod est, nulli est iniuste nocendum, sequitur non esse furandum; quod quidem ad naturale pertinet. *Alio modo* oritur aliquid ex iusto naturali per modum determinationis; et sic omnia iusta positiva vel legalia ex iusto naturali oriuntur. Sicut furem esse puniendum est iustum naturale; sed quod sit etiam puniendus tali

103

vel tali poena, hoc est legale positivum." *In decem libros*, 280. The English translation appears in *Commentary on Aristotle's Nocomachean Ethics*, 326.

7. The text is from 3.129: "Praeterea. Quorumcumque est natura determinata, oportet esse operationes determinatas, quae illi naturae conveniant: propria enim operatio uniuscuiusque naturam ipsius sequitur. Constat autem hominum naturam esse determinatam. Oportet igitur esse aliquas operationes secundum se homini convenientes.

Adhuc. Cuicumque est aliquid naturale, oportet esse naturale id sine quo illud haberi non potest: *natura* enim *non deficit in nessariis.* Est autem homini naturale quod sit *animal sociale* : quod ex hoc ostenditur, quia unus homo solus non sufficit ad omnia quae sunt humanae vitae necessaria. Ea igitur sine quibus societas humana conservari non potest, sunt homini naturaliter convenientia. Huiusmodi autem sunt, unicuique quod suum est conservare, et ab iniuriis abstinere. Sunt igitur aliqua in humanis actibus naturaliter recta." From *Liber de Veritate Catholicae Fidei contra errores Indidelium seu Summa Contra Gentiles*, ed. Petro Caramello, Petro Marc, OSB, and Ceslai Pera, OP (Rome: Marietti, 1961), 3:191. English translation from St. Thomas Aquinas, *Summa Contra Gentiles, Book Three: Providence*, part 2, trans. Vernon J. Bourke (Notre Dame, Ind.: University of Notre Dame Press, 1975), 163.

8. John Locke, *Essays on the Law of Nature*, ed. W. von Leyden (Oxford: Clarendon Press, 1988), 111.

9. Leo Strauss, *What Is Political Philosophy?* (Chicago: University of Chicago Press, 1988), 197.

10. Ibid., 218.

11. "Deontological" morality is rooted in *deon* (duty), while *on* (being) provides the foundation for "ontological" morality. For a succinct discussion of Kantian deontological morality, see Henry B. Veatch, *For An Ontology of Morals: A Critique of Contemporary Ethical Theory* (Evanston, Ill.: Northwestern University Press, 1971), 145–152.

12. See Brian Tierney, *The Idea of Natural Rights* (Atlanta: Scholars Press, 1997). Tierney, perhaps more than any other scholar working today, has shown that already in the Middle Ages there were important debates about rights. He has also demonstrated how the political thought of William of Ockham prepared the way for early modern theories of natural rights. See pages 157–203. While I do not agree with some of Tierney's conclusions (for example, his reading in some instances of *ius* as right in the modern sense), his research is absolutely fundamental for medieval rights theory.

13. See especially *Summa Theologiae* 1–2, q. 122, art. 6.

14. See John Finnis, *Aquinas: Moral, Political, and Legal Theory* (Oxford: Oxford University Press, 1998).

15. The history of Platonic thought provides a very good example. For centuries, Plato is known almost exclusively through the works of the Neoplatonists rather than from Plato's own texts. In the fifteenth century, the

Florentine Neoplatonist Marsilio Ficino made many of the works of Plato accessible to Western Europe for the first time since the time of Boethius. See Brian P. Copenhaver and Charles B. Schmitt, *Renaissance Philosophy* (Oxford: Oxford University Press, 1992), 127–146.

16. The standard English biography of Suárez is that of Joseph H. Fichter, *Man of Spain: Francis Suárez* (New York: Macmillan, 1940). For a very brief but accurate biographical sketch, see John P. Doyle, "Francisco Suárez: On Preaching the Gospel to People Like the American Indians," *Fordham International Law Journal* 15, no. 4 (1991–92): 881–884.

17. See Charles H. Lohr, "*Metaphysics*," in *The Cambridge History of Renaissance Philosophy*, ed. Charles B. Schmitt and Quentin Skinner (Cambridge: Cambridge University Press, 1988), 615.

18. For a discussion of the most important Thomists of Leo's day, see Gerald A. McCool, SJ, *The Neo-Thomists* (Milwaukee: Marquette University Press, 1994), 30–34.

19. It is very hard to know with certainty how much Leo was influenced by the Suarezians. While it is true that Leo was surrounded by Suarezians, it must be noted that he almost never mentions Suárez in his encyclicals. In *Aeterni Patris*, the commentator Leo mentions with approval is Cajetan (Thomas De Vio, 1469–1534), a Dominican. When the Leonine edition of the *Summa Theologiae* was prepared, Cajetan's commentary was published along with Thomas's text.

20. See Leonard E. Boyle, OP, "A Remembrance of Pope Leo XIII: The Encyclical Aeterni Patris," in *One Hundred Years of Thomism*, ed. Victor B. Brezik, CSB (Houston: Center for Thomistic Studies, 1981), 11.

21. The revival of Thomism had already started in the mid-nineteenth century; what Leo did was to endorse Thomism as the "official" philosophy of the Roman Church. Obviously, Leo did not know that *Aeterni Patris* would inspire several different schools of Thomistic thought that eventually would become philosophical and theological rivals. For a very informative examination of these rival schools, see Gerald A. McCool, SJ, *From Unity to Pluralism: The Internal Evolution of Thomism* (New York: Fordham University Press, 1989).

Chapter 1: Thomistic Ontology

1. Aristotle, *Metaphysics*, book 4, 1. *The Complete Works of Aristotle*, ed. Jonathan Barnes (Princeton, N.J.: Princeton University Press, 1984), 2:1584.

2. Werner Beierwaltes, "Image and Counterimage: Reflections on Neoplatonic Thought with Respect to Its Place today," in *Neoplatonism and Early Christian Thought*, ed. H. J. Blumenthal and R. A. Markus (London: Variorum Publications, 1981), 237–238.

3. Joseph Owens, *The Doctrine of Being in the Aristotelian "Metaphysics"* (Toronto: Pontifical Institute of Mediaeval Studies, 1978), 292.

4. "Ipsum esse est perfectissimum omnium, comparatur enim ad omnia ut actus. Nihil enim habet actualitatem nisi inquantum est, unde ipsum esse est actualitas omnium rerum et etiam ipsarum formarum. Unde non comparatur ad alia sicut recipiens ad receptum, sed magis sicut receptum ad recipiens. Cum enim dico esse hominis vel equi vel cujuscumque alterius, ipsum esse consideratur ut formale et receptum, non autem illud cui competit esse." *Summa theologiae* 1, q. 4, art. 1. (All quotes from this text, hereafter abbreviated *ST,* will be taken from the Blackfriars edition.) The English translation appears on page 51. It is also true that for St. Thomas existence and goodness are very closely linked: "Inasmuch as they exist, all things are good. For everything, inasmuch as it exists, is actual and therefore in some way perfect, all actuality being a sort of perfection. Now we have shown above that anything perfect is desirable and good. It follows then that, inasmuch as they exist, all things are good." The Latin text reads, "Omne ens inquantum est ens est bonum. Omne enim ens inquantum est ens est in actu et quodammodo perfectum, quia omnis actus perfectio quaedam est. Perfectum vero habet rationem appetibilis et boni, ut ex dictis patet. Unde sequitur omne ens inquantum hujusmodi bonum esse." *ST* 1, q. 5, art. 3. See also *Quaestiones Disputatae de Veritate,* q. 21, art. 2.

5. Etienne Gilson, *Being and Some Philosophers,* 2nd ed. (Toronto: Pontifical Institute of Mediaeval Studies, 1952), 188–189. See also John F. Wippel, *The Metaphysical Thought of Thomas Aquinas* (Washington, D.C.: Catholic University of America Press, 2000), 31–33.

6. See James A. Weisheipl, OP, *Friar Thomas D'Aquino: His Life, Thought, and Work* (New York: Doubleday, 1974), 335–338.

7. Ibid., 338–343.

8. Some scholars, in fact, have argued that Ockham's influence continued into the seventeenth and eighteenth centuries. See Julius R. Weinberg, *A Short History of Medieval Philosophy* (Princeton, N.J.: Princeton University Press, 1964), 265.

9. "Et quia tactum est de esse existere, aliquantulum disgrediendo considerandum est, qualiter esse existere se habet ad rem: Utrum esse rei et essentia rei sint duo extra animam distincta inter se. Et mihi videtur, quod non sunt talia duo, nec 'esse existere' significat aliquid distinctum a re. Quia si sic, aut esset substantia aut accidens. Non accidens, quia tunc esse existere hominis esset qualitas vel quantitas, quod est manifeste falsum. . . . Nec potest dici, quod sit substantia: quia omnis substantia vel est materia vel forma vel compositum, vel substantia absoluta; sed manifestum est, quod nullum istorum potest dici esse, si esse sit alia res ab entitate rei. Item si essent duae res, aut facerent per se unum, aut non. Si sic, oporteret quod unum esset actus et reliquum potentia, et per consequens unum esset materia et aliud forma, quod est absurdum. . . . Ideo dicendum est, quod entitas et existentia non sunt duae res. Sed ista duo vocabula 'res' et 'esse' idem et eadem significant, sed unum nominaliter et aliud verbaliter." *Summa Totius Logicae* 3, 2, 27.

Latin text and English translation from *Ockham: Philosophical Writings*, ed. Philotheus Boehner (London: Nelson, 1962), 92–93.

10. David Knowles, *The Evolution of Medieval Thought* (London: Longmans, 1962), 333.

11. Anthony Kenny, *A New History of Western Philosophy*, vol. 2, *Medieval Philosophy* (Oxford: Clarendon Press, 2005), 275.

12. Frederick Copleston, SJ, *A History of Philosophy*, vol. 3, *Late Medieval and Renaissance Philosophy*, part 1 (New York: Image Books, 1963), 161–162. For a discussion of how Capreolus's philosophy differs from that of St. Thomas, see Norman J. Wells, "Capreolus on Essence and Existence," *The Modern Schoolman* 38 (1960): 1–24.

13. See Melquíades Andrés, *La teología española en el siglo XVI* (Madrid: Biblioteca de Autores Cristianos, 1977), 2:331–332.

14. Francisco Peccorini, "Knowledge of the Singular: Aquinas, Suarez, and Recent Interpreters," *The Thomist* 38 (1974): 606.

15. Dominic Bañez, *The Primacy of Existence in Thomas Aquinas*, trans. Benjamin S. Llamzon (Chicago: Regnery, 1966), 34–35. The Latin text reads, "Existentia aliquid reale est, et intrinsecum rei existenti . . . quia existentia est id quo res constituitur extra nihil . . . quoniam existentia est prima actualitas per quam res educitur extra nihil; ergo debet esse intima rei, alias inintelligibile est quomodo res sit extra nihil, per aliquam rationem quae sit extra rem. Confirmatur: quoniam si prima actualitas uniuscujusque rei esset extrinseca, nulla alia actualitas posset esse intrinseca. Probatur sequela: quoniam prima actualitas est fundamentum aliarum." Dominico Báñes, *Scholastica Commentaria in Primam Partem Summae Theologicae S. Thomae Aquinatis*, ed. Luis Urgano, OP (Madrid: Editorial FEDA, 1934), 143.

16. Peccorini, "Knowledge of the Singular," 606–607.

17. See José Ferrater Mora, "Suarez and Modern Philosophy," *Journal of the History of Ideas* 14 (1953): 537–541.

18. Joseph Owens, CSSR, "The Number of Terms in the Suarezian Discussion of Essence and Being," *The Modern Schoolman* 35 (1957): 174.

19. John P. Doyle, "Suarez On the Reality of the Possibles," *The Modern Schoolman* 45 (1967): 36–37.

20. David M. Knight, SJ, "Suarez's Approach to Substantial Form," *The Modern Schoolman* 40 (1962): 238.

21. "Dicendum ergo est eamdem rem esse essentiam et existentiam, concipi autem sub ratione essentiae, quatenus ratione eius constituitur res sub tali genere et specie. Est enim essentia, ut supra . . . declaravimus, id quo primo aliquid constituitur intra latitudinem entis realis, ut distinguitur ab ente ficto, et in unoquoque particulari ente essentia eius dicitur id ratione cuius in tali gradu et ordine entim constituitur." Francisco Suárez, *Disputaciones metafísicas*, ed. and trans. Sergio Rábade Romeo, Salvador Caballero Sánchez, and Antonio Puigcerver Zanón (Madrid, Biblioteca Hispánica de Filosofía,

1963), 5:71. The English translation is that of Norman Wells, found in *Francis Suárez On the Essence of Finite Being As Such, On the Existence of That Essence and Their Distinction* (Milwaukee: Marquette University Press, 1983), 102.

22. "We said, then, that we can speak of the principle of individuation in two ways: First, with respect to being and to the proper constitution of a thing in itself; second, with respect to production, insofar as the agent is determined to produce a distinct individual or to cause one rather than another, and, consequently, with respect to our knowledge insofar as sensibly—if I may put it so—we can distinguish one from another. Therefore, according to the former consideration—which is the most *a priori*, and the most proper to this science—the second view is true, the one that teaches that accidents do not have their individuation and numerical distinction from the subject, but from their proper entities." Disputation V, section vii. English translation from *Suarez On Individuation, Metaphysical Disputation V: Individual Unity and Its Principle*, ed. Jorge J. E. Gracia (Milwaukee: Marquette University Press, 1982), 141–142. The Latin text reads, "Diximus enim dupliciter posse nos loqui de principio individuationis: primo, in ordine ad esse et ad propriam rei constitutionem secundum se. Secundo, in ordine ad productionem, quatenus determinatur agens ad distinctum individuum producendum, vel ad efficiendum unum potius quam aliud, et consequenter in ordine ad nostram cognitionem quatenus sensibiliter (ut sic dicam) distinguere possumus unum ab alio. Priori igitur consideratione (quae maxime a priori est, et maxime propria huius scientiae), vera est posterior sententia, docens accidentia non ex subiecto, sed ex propriis entitatibus habere suam individuationem et numericam distinctionem." *Disputaciones metafísicas*, 1:666.

23. The distinction between essence and existence was already known by philosophers from the time of Aristotle, who himself talks about this difference in *Posterior Analytics* 2, 7. For a brief overview of the history of this question, see Leo J. Elders, *The Metaphysics of Being of St. Thomas Aquinas in a Historical Perspective* (Leiden: E. J. Brill, 1993), 170–174.

24. Ralph McInerny, *Boethius and Aquinas* (Washington, D.C.: Catholic University of America Press, 1990), 199–231. See also *Praeambula Fidei: Thomism and the God of the Philosophers* (Washington, D.C.: Catholic University of America Press, 2006), 144–150.

25. "Dicendum quod necesse est dicere omne quod quocumque modo est a Deo est. Si enim aliquid invenitur in aliquo per participationem, necesse est quod causetur in ipso ab eo cui essentialiter convenit; sicut ferrum fit ignitum ab igne. Ostensum est autem supra . . . quod Deus est ipsum esse per se subsistens. . . . Relinquitur ergo quod omnia alia a Deo non sint suum esse, sed participant esse." *ST* 1, q. 44, art. 1.

26. "Cum autem Deus sit ipsum esse per suam essentiam oportet quod esse creatum sit proprius effectus ejus, sicut igniri est proprius effectus ignis. Hunc autem effectum causat Deus in rebus non solum quando primo esse

incipiunt sed quamdiu in esse conservantur, sicut lumen causatur in aere a sole quamdiu aer illuminatus manet. Quamdiu igitur res habet esse tamdiu oportet quod Deus adsit ei secundum modum quo esse habet. Esse autem est illud quod est magis intimum cuilibet et quod profundius omnibus inest, cum sit formale respectu omnium quae in re sunt, ut ex supra dictis patet. Unde oportet quod Deus sit in omnibus rebus et intime." *ST* 1, q. 8, art. 1. See also *De Veritate*, q. 22, art. 2.

27. One of the clearest examples of this point can be found in St. Thomas's discussion of Creation in book 2 of the *Summa Contra Gentiles*. Chapters 15 and 16 are of special interest in this regard. An excellent commentary on these chapters is that of Norman Kretzmann, *The Metaphysics of Creation* (Oxford: Clarendon Press, 1999), 53–87.

28. One important exception to this general tendency can be observed in the ongoing debate concerning "natural kinds." T. E. Wilkerson, in his fascinating book *Natural Kinds* (Aldershot: Avebury, 1995), has stated, "There are natural kinds. Each natural kind is determined by a real essence, a property or set of properties necessary and sufficient for membership of the kind. The real essence in turn determines the causal powers of individual members of the kind. Biological natural kinds are determined by genetic real essences which causally affect the structure and behavior of individual members of the kind. But, since there is considerable interspecific genetic similarity and intraspecific genetic variation, there are far more biological natural kinds than species" (133). Clearly, Wilkerson defends the notion that at least some knowledge of the world as it really exists is attainable. My point is that Wilkerson and those who would defend this position represent the exception rather than the general rule in modern philosophy.

Chapter 2: Ontological Morality and Human Rights

1. Ernest L. Fortin, *Human Rights, Virtue, and the Common Good: Untimely Meditations on Religion and Politics* (Lanham, Md.: Rowman and Littlefield, 1996), 115.

2. "Dicendum quod de bono et malo in actionibus oportet loqui sicut de bono et malo in rebus, eo quod unaquaeque res talem actionem producit, qualis est ipsa. In rebus autem unumquodque tantum habet de bono quantum habet de esse; bonum enim et ens convertuntur. . . .

"Sic igitur dicendum est quod omnis actio, inquantum habet aliquid de esse intantum habet de bonitate; inquantum vero deficit ei aliquid de plenitudine essendi quae debetur actioni humanae intantum deficit a bonitate, et sic dicitur mala: puta, si deficiat ei vel determinata quantitas secundum rationem, vel debitus locus, vel aliquid hujusmodi." (*Summa Theologiae* 1–2, q. 18 art, 1; all quotes are taken from the Blackfriars edition.)

3. Jan A. Aertsen, "Thomas Aquinas on the Good: The Relation Between Metaphysics and Ethics," in *Aquinas's Moral Theory*, ed. Scott MacDonald

and Eleonore Stump (Ithaca, N.Y.: Cornell University Press, 1999), 250. See also *ST* 1, q. 79, art. 11. It must be stated, however, that many scholars do not accept this interpretation of Aquinas's thought. In particular, mention should be made of Germain G. Grisez. In his seminal article "The First Principle of Practical Reason: A Commentary on the *Summa theologiae*, 1–2, Question 94, Article 2" (*Natural Law Forum* 10:168–201), Grisez defends a notion of the autonomy of practical reason. For Grisez, practical reason does not proceed from theoretical reason; rather, it is itself based on *per se nota* first principles. Grisez's thesis has had a major impact on one important school (consisting of Grisez, Boyle, and Finnis) of current research on natural-law theory. For a critique of this thesis, see Ralph McInerny, "The Primacy of Theoretical Knowledge: Some Remarks on John Finnis," in *Aquinas on Human Action* (Washington, D.C: Catholic University of America Press, 1992), 184–192.

4. " . . . et talis cognitio finis competit soli rationali naturae. Imperfecta autem cognitio finis est quae in sola finis apprehensione consistit, sine hoc quod cognoscatur ratio finis et proportio actus ad finem; et talis cognitio finis reperitur in brutis animalibus per sensum et aestimationem naturalem.

"Perfectam igitur cognitionem finis sequitur voluntarium secundum rationem perfectam, prout scilicet apprehenso fine aliquis potest deliberans de fine et de his quae sunt ad finem, moveri in finem vel non moveri" (*ST* 1–2, q. 6, art 2).

5. For a very good discussion of this point, see Fred D. Miller Jr., *Nature, Justice, and Rights in Aristotle's Politics* (Oxford: Oxford University Press, 1995), 132–133.

6. " . . . ultima et perfecta beatitudo non potest esse nisi in visione divinae essentiae." *ST* 1–2, q. 3, art. 89. Also: "Erit igitur ultima felicitas hominis in cognitione Dei quam habet humana mens post hanc vitam, per modum quo ipsum cognoscunt substantiae separatae." *Summa Contra Gentiles*, book 3, chapter 48.

7. "Dicendum quod aliquis homo dupliciter considerari potest: uno modo secundum se; alio modo per comparationem ad aliud. Secundum se quidem considerando hominem, nullum occidere licet, quia in quolibet etiam peccatore debemus amare naturam quam Deus fecit, quae per occisionem corrumpitur. Sed, sicut supra dictum est, occisio peccatoris fit licita per comparationem ad bonum commune, quod per peccatum corrumpitur. Vita autem justorum est conservativa et promotiva boni communis, quia ipsi sunt principalior pars multitudinis. Et ideo nullo modo licet occidere innocentem." (*ST* 2–2, q. 64 , art. 6.)

8. *Politics* 7.16.1335b 20–25, *The Complete Works of Aristotle*, ed. Jonathan Barnes (Princeton, N.J.: Princeton University Press, 1984), 2:2119. All quotes are taken from this edition.

9. *Magna Moralia* 1.4.1185a 1–5, 2:1873.

10. *Politics* 12.12.1260a 7–15, 2:1999.

11. *Physics* 2.8.199a 34–199b 4, 1:340.

12. John Finnis, *Aquinas: Moral, Political, and Legal Theory* (Oxford: Oxford University Press, 1998), 136–137.

13. "Dicendum quod justitiae proprium est inter alias virtutes ut ordinet hominem in his quae sunt ad alterum. Importat enim aequalitatem quamdam, ut ipsum nomen demonstrat: dicuntur enim vulgariter ea quae adaequantur justari; aequalitas autem ad alterum est. Aliae autem virtutes perficiunt hominem solum in his quae ei conveniunt secundum seipsum. . . . Sic ergo justum dicitur aliquid quasi habens rectitudinem justitiae, ad quod terminatur actio justitiae etiam non considerato qualiter ab agente fiat. Sed in aliis virtutibus non determinatur aliquid rectum nisi secundum quod aliqualiter fit ab agente. Et propter hoc specialiter justitiae prae aliis virtutibus determinatur secundum se objectum, quod vocatur justum; et hoc quidem est jus. Unde manifestum est quod jus est objectum justitiae" (*ST* 2–2, q. 57, art. 1). For a brief explanation of Thomas's objective sense of the term *ius*, see Annabel S. Brett, *Liberty, Right and Nature: Individual Rights in Later Scholastic Thought* (Cambridge: Cambridge University Press, 1997), 90–94.

14. *Rhetoric* 1.13.1373b 1–11, 2:2187.

15. The Latin text reads, "Ius namque idem est (ut ait lib. 5. Isid.) quod iustum. Est enim objectum iustitiae: puta aequitas quam iustitia inter homines constituit: dominium autem facultas est domini (uti nomen sonat) in servos vel in res, quibus suo arbitratu, ob suumque commodum utitur. Fit ergo, ut ius non convertatur cum dominio, sed sit illi superius and latius patens." Both texts may be found in Richard Tuck, *Natural Rights Theories* (Cambridge: Cambridge University Press, 1979), 47.

16. Brian Tierney, *The Idea of Natural Rights* (Atlanta: Scholars Press, 1997), 265.

17. Ibid., 259.

18. More radical than Tierney's position on this question is that of Marcelo Sánchez-Sorondo, who argues, "in the history of the progressive consciousness of the human person, his rights, and his duties, Francisco de Vitoria appears as the original philosopher of rights." See "Vitoria: The Original Philosopher of Rights," in *Hispanic Philosophy in the Age of Discovery*, ed. Kevin White (Washington, D.C.: Catholic University of America Press, 1997), 67.

19. The Latin text reads, "Et per haec satisfieri illis debet, qui sciscitantur utrum iure naturalis dominii possimus Christiani infideles armis infestare, qui pro suorum morum ruditate, naturales videntur esse servi. Nullum enim inde ius contra eos acquirimus vi illos subiugandi. Eo quod servitus illa libertatem non tollit, veluti illorum conditio, qui vel se vendiderunt, vel bello capti sunt." Domingo de Soto, *De la justicia y del derecho* (Madrid: Instituto de Estudios Políticos, 1968), 2:290 (English translation mine).

20. *Politics* 1.8.1256b 20–25, 2:1993–1994.

21. For Soto's competence as a natural scientist, see *The Cambridge History of Renaissance Philosophy*, ed. Charles B. Schmitt and Quentin Skinner (Cambridge: Cambridge University Press, 1988), 221–228.

22. Annabel S. Brett, *Liberty, Right and Nature: Individual Rights in Later Scholastic Thought* (Cambridge: Cambridge University Press, 1997), 154.

23. Ibid., 163.

24. The Latin text reads, "Et iuxta posteriorem, et strictam iuris significationem solet proprie ius vocari facultas quaedam moralis, quam unusquisque habet, vel circa rem suam, vel ad rem sibi debitam; sic enim dominus rei dicitur habere ius in re, et operarius dicitur habbere ius ad stipendium ratione cuius dicitur dignus mercede sua. Et haec significatio vocis huius frequens est non solum in iure, sed itiam in scriptura . . . illa ergo actio, seu moralis facultas, quam unusquisque habet ad rem suam, vel ad rem ad se aliquo modo pertinentem vocatur ius, et illud proprie videtur esse obiectum iustitie." From *Tractatus de Legibus, ac Deo Legislatore*, book 1, chapter 2, section 5. The Latin text appears in Francisco Suárez, *Selections from Three Works of Francisco Suárez, S.J.* (Oxford: Clarendon Press, 1944), 1:11. The English translation by Gwladys L. Williams et al. is found in 2:30–31.

25. Hugo Grotius, *The Law of War and Peace*, trans. Francis W. Kelsey (New York: Bobbs-Merrill, 1925), 35–36.

26. J. B. Schneewind, *The Invention of Autonomy: A History of Modern Moral Philosophy* (Cambridge: Cambridge University Press, 1998), 81.

27. Grotius, *Law of War and Peace*, 36.

28. Peter J. Stanlis, *Edmund Burke and the Natural Law* (Ann Arbor: University of Michigan Press, 1958), 19.

Chapter 3: The War of the Philosophers

1. Charles H. Lohr, *Latin Aristotle Commentaries*, vol. 2, *Renaissance Authors* (Florence: Leo S. Olschki, 1988).

2. Walter Bernard Redmond, *Bibliography of the Philosophy in the Iberian Colonies of America* (The Hague: Nijhoff, 1972).

3. Angel Losada, *Juan Ginés de Sepúlveda a través de su "Epistolario" y nuevos documentos* (Madrid: Consejo Superior de Investigaciones Científicas, 1973), 33.

4. Lohr, *Latin Aristotle Commentaries*, 80.

5. Otis H. Green, "A Note on Spanish Humanism: Sepúlveda and his Translation of Aristotle's *Politics*," *Hispanic Review* 8 (1940): 340.

6. Juan Ginés de Sepúlveda, *Demócrates Segundo o de las justas causas de la guerra contra los indios*, ed. Angel Losada (Madrid: Consejo Superior de Investigaciones Científicas, 1984), xx–xxi.

7. Aristotle, *Politics* 1.5.1254b–1255a, text from *The Complete Works of Aristotle*, ed. Jonathan Barnes (Princeton, N.J.: Princeton University Press, 1985), 2:1990–1991.

8. Sepúlveda, *Demócrates segundo*, 19–22 (English translation mine).

9. Lohr, *Latin Aristotle Commentaries*, 430–431.

10. The Latin texts reads, "Nullum ius potest naturali derogare: naturali autem omnes homines nascuntur liberi . . . servitus sit qua quis dominio alieno contra naturam subiicitur. Et Gregorio idem asserere ubi ait contra naturam esse homines hominibus dominari: rationeque idem monstrante: nam homo eo caeteris animantibus praestat quod ratione viget et libertatis arbitrio." Domingo de Soto, *De la justicia y del derecho*, ed. Marcelino González, OP, and Venancio Diego Carro, OP (Madrid: Instituto de Estudios Políticos, 1968), 2:288 (English translation mine).

11. "Servitutem esse contra naturam: nempe contra primam naturae intentionem, qua cupit omnes homines secundum rationem studiosos esse. At tamen illa deficiente intentione, ex culpa subsequuta est poena, quae est conformis naturae corruptae. Atque inter poenarum genera unum est legalis servitus." *De Iustitia et Iure*, book 4, q. 2, art. 2. Ibid., 290.

12. Bartolomé de Las Casas, *In Defense of the Indians*, trans. and ed. Stafford Poole, CM (DeKalb: Northern Illinois University Press, 1992), 42.

13. J. H. Elliott, "The Spanish Conquest and Settlement in America," in *The Cambridge History of Latin America*, ed. Leslie Bethell (Cambridge: Cambridge University Press, 1984), 1:167.

14. Francisco de Vitoria, *Political Writings*, ed. Anthony Pagden and Jeremy Lawrance (Cambridge: Cambridge University Press, 1991), 233.

15. Ibid., 251.

16. Brian Tierney, *The Idea of Natural Rights* (Atlanta: Scholars Press, 1997), 271.

17. José de Acosta, *De Procuranda Indorum Salute*, ed. V. Abril, C. Baciero, J. Barrientos, A García, F. Maseda, L. Pereña, and D. Ramos (Madrid: Consejo Superior de Investigaciones Científicas, 1984), 293.

18. Lohr, *Latin Aristotle Commentaries*, 32.

19. Vitoria, *Political Writings*, 63.

20. Ibid., 263.

21. Francisco Suárez, *A Work on the Three Theological Virtues: Faith, Hope and Charity*, in *Selections From Three Words of Francisco Suárez, S.J.*, ed. James Brown Scott (Oxford: Clarendon Press, 1944), 768.

22. Ibid., 768–769.

23. Ibid., 771.

24. Bartolomé de Las Casas, *De Unico Vocationis Modo*, in *Obras Completas*, ed. Paulino Castañeda and Antonio García del Moral, OP (Madrid: Alianza Editorial, 1990), 2:20.

25. Las Casas, *In Defense of the Indians*, 39.

26. Melchor Cano, *De Dominio Indiorum*, in *Misión de España en América*, ed. Vicente Luciano Pereña (Madrid: Consejo Superior de Investigaciones Científicas, 1956), 102.

27. Jean-Pierre Torrell places the work between 1269 and 1272 during the second Paris period. See Jean-Pierre Torrell, OP, *Saint Thomas Aquinas*, trans. Robert Royal (Washington, D.C.: Catholic University of America Press, 1996), 1:344.

28. Thomas's commentary ends at 3.6.1280a6. See James A. Weisheipl, OP, *Friar Thomas D'Aquino: His Life, Thought, and Works* (Washington, D.C.: Catholic University of America Press, 1983), 380–381.

29. Harry V. Jaffa, *Thomism and Aristotelianism: A Study of the Commentary by Thomas Aquinas on the Nicomachean Ethics* (Westport, Conn.: Greenwood Press, 1979), 186–188. It should be noted here that there is indeed a short passage about slavery in the commentary on the *Ethics*, but, once again, St. Thomas merely clarifies the position presented in Aristotle's text.

30. "Hunc hominem esse servum, absolute considerando, magis quam alium, non habet rationem naturalem, sed solum secundum aliquam utilitatem consequentem, inquantum utile est huic quod regatur a sapientiori, et illi quod ad hoc juvetur, ut dicitur in *Pol*. Et ideo servitus pertinens ad jus gentium est naturalis secundo modo, sed non primo modo." (All quotes are taken from the Blackfriars edition.)

31. "Duplex est subjectio; una servilis, secundum quam praesidens utitur subjecto ad sui ipsius utilitatem, et talis sujectio introducta est post peccatum. Est autem alia subjectio oeconomica vel civilis, secundum quam praesidens utitur subjectis ad eorum utiltatem et bonum. Et ista subjectio fuisset etiam ante peccatum. Defuisset enim bonum ordinis in humana multitudine si quidam per alios sapientiores gubernati non fuissent."

32. "Servus in hoc differt a libero quod *liber est causa sui* ut dicitur in principio *Meta*.; servus autem ordinatur ad alterum. Tunc ergo aliquis dominatur alicui ut servo quando eum cui dominatur ad propriam utilitatem sui, scilicet dominantis, refert. Et quia unicuique est appetibile proprium bonum, et per consequens contristabile est unicuique quod illud bonum quod deberet esse suum cedat alteri tantum; ideo tale dominium non potest esse sine poena subjectorum. Propter quod in statu innocentiae non fuisset tale dominium hominis ad hominem."

33. "Aliquid dicitur esse de jure naturali dupliciter: uno modo, quia ad hoc natura inclinat, sicut non esse injuriam alteri faciendam; alio modo, quia natura non inducit contrarium, sicut possemus dicere quod hominem esse nudum est de jure naturali, quia natura non debit ei vestitum, sed ars adinvenit. Et hoc modo communis omnium possessio et una libertas dicitur esse de jure naturali, quia scilicet distinctio possessionum et servitus non sunt inductae a natura, sed per hominum rationem ad utilitatem humanae vitae."

34. "Tenetur autem homo homini obedire in his quae exterius per corpus sunt agenda; in quibus tamen secundum ea quae ad naturam corporis pertinent, homo homini obedire non tenetur, sed solum Deo, quia omnes homines natura sunt pares, puta in his quae pertinent ad corporis sustentationem et

prolis generationem. Unde non tenentur nec servi dominis nec filii parentibus obedire de matrimonio contrahendo vel virginitate servanda aut aliquo alio hujusmodi. Sed in his quae pertinent ad dispositionem actuum et rerum humanarum tenetur subditus suo superiori obedire secundum rationem superioritatis; sicut miles duci exercitus in his quae pertinent ad bellum, servus domino in his quae pertinent ad servilia opera exequenda." In the following article (q. 104, art. 6) Thomas provides what almost seems like a qualification of article 5. In article 6, Thomas stresses the importance of obedience to human law. My view is that this clarification does not change the fact that in article 5 Thomas stresses personal freedom.

35. Vitoria, *Political Writings*, xxxii.

36. Charles H. Lohr, "Metaphysics," in *The Cambridge History of Renaissance Philosophy*, ed. Charles B. Schmitt and Quentin Skinner (Cambridge: Cambridge University Press, 1988), 615–620.

37. Some may argue that precisely what Grotius did was to break with the late Scholastics; however, it is clear that Grotius inherited much from this earlier tradition. For an excellent discussion of this issue, see James Gordley, *The Philosophical Origins of Modern Contract Doctrine* (Oxford: Clarendon Press, 1991), 121–132.

38. Anthony Pagden, *The Fall of Natural Man* (Cambridge: Cambridge University Press, 1982), 104–105.

39. Ibid., 117–118.

40. Ibid., 111.

Chapter 4: The Modern Way

1. John Locke, *Epistola de Tolerantia: A Letter on Toleration*, ed. Raymond Klibansky (Oxford: Clarendon Press, 1968), ix.

2. Ibid., 71.

3. See Nicholas Wolterstorff, "Locke's Philosophy of Religion," in *The Cambridge Companion to Locke*, ed. Vere Chappell (Cambridge: Cambridge University Press, 1994), 185.

4. Locke, *Epistola*, 85–87.

5. See *Church and State Through the Centuries*, ed. Sidney Z. Ehler and John B. Morrall (London: Burns and Oates, 1954), 208–213.

6. Locke, *Epistola*, 113.

7. Ibid., 133.

8. For a brief summary of the conflict, see James Brodrick, SJ, *Robert Bellarmine, Saint and Scholar* (London: Burns and Oates, 1961), 264–302. Bellarmine was not alone in his criticism of King James. Francisco Suárez had also challenged the authority of the English monarch in his *Defensio fidei*, published in 1613.

9. Pope Pius IX, *Quanta Cura*, in *Papal Encyclicals, 1740–1878*, ed. Claudia Carlen Ihm (Ann Arbor: Pierian Press, 1981), 1:382.

10. See Ehler and Morall, *Church and State*, 254–270.

11. Louis Dupré, *Passage to Modernity* (New Haven: Yale University Press, 1993), 143.

12. Immanuel Kant, *Practical Philosophy*, ed. and trans. Mary J. Gregor (Cambridge: Cambridge University Press, 1996), 387.

13. Ibid., 389.

14. Ibid., 389–390.

15. Ibid., 393–394.

16. Ibid., 432.

17. Ibid.

18. Ibid., 473.

19. Gottfried Dietze, *Liberalism Proper and Proper Liberalism* (Baltimore: Johns Hopkins University Press, 1985), 149.

20. Kant, *Practical Philosophy*, 474.

21. Ibid., 475.

22. Max Scheler, *Formalism in Ethics and Non-Formal Ethics of Values: A New Attempt Toward the Foundation of an Ethical Personalism*, trans. Manfred S. Frings and Rober L. Funk (Evanston, Ill.: Northwestern University Press, 1973), pp. 226–227.

23. J. B. Schneewind, *The Invention of Autonomy: A History of Modern Moral Philosophy* (Cambridge: Cambridge University Press, 1998), 483.

24. Writing in the early twentieth century from an Orthodox Jewish perspective, Isaac Breuer stated the following concerning moral autonomy and its implications for modern law: "Autonomous ethics demands of me that I should act 'properly.' However, I can only act 'properly' when the causal intention of my action is proper. The law does not demand that I should act 'properly,' but that I should act 'lawfully,' that I should give obedience to the statutes of law. But since the law is one that has been laid down by men, the obedience given to the law must be in itself ethically completely indifferent. Autonomous ethics cannot therefore make the maxims concrete for modern law, nor can modern law effect autonomously ethical action on the part of those subject to the law. Law and ethics go their separate ways and only by way of defining boundaries does ethics block the path of legal monstrosities." This article (published originally in German in 1910) appears in English translation in Isaac Breuer, *Concepts of Judaism*, ed. Jacob S. Levinger (Jerusalem: Israel Universities Press, 1974), 76–77. Rabbi Breuer's position is very similar to the view that would be defended later by Roman Catholic leaders and by thinkers from other traditions who defend an older, "premodern" ontological morality.

25. Henry B. Veatch, *For an Ontology of Morals: A Critique of Contemporary Ethical Theory* (Evanston, Ill.: Northwestern University Press, 1971), 150.

26. With this remark I certainly do not mean to suggest that Kant was the first or the only philosopher in his day to propose a moral system without

an ontological foundation. In 1751, David Hume (1711–1776), the sworn enemy of metaphysics, had argued that the sole basis for justice is utility: "Thus, the rules of equity or justice depend entirely on the particular state and condition in which men are placed, and owe their origin and existence to that Utility, which results to the public from their strict and regular observance. Reverse, in any considerable circumstance, the condition of men: Produce extreme abundance or extreme necessity: Implant in the human breast perfect moderation and humanity, or perfect rapaciousness and malice: By rendering justice totally *useless*, you thereby totally destroy its essence, and suspend its obligation upon mankind." David Hume, *An Enquiry Concerning the Principles of Morals*, ed. Tom L. Beauchamp (Oxford: Oxford University Press, 1998), 86. It is not an accident that both Kant and Hume have had a powerful impact on philosophers in the analytical tradition. One especially attractive feature for these philosophers is the "objectivity of moral rules" that they encounter in Kant's thought, as Alasdair MacIntyre has observed: "Such analytical philosophers revived the Kantian project of demonstrating that the authority and objectivity of moral rules is precisely that authority and objectivity which belongs to the exercise of reason. Hence their central project was, indeed is, that of showing that any rational agent is logically committed to the rules of morality in virtue of his or her rationality." Alasdair MacIntyre, *After Virtue* (Notre Dame, Ind.: University of Notre Dame Press, 1984), 66.

27. G. W. F. Hegel, *Elements of the Philosophy of Right*, ed. Allen W. Wood, trans. H. B. Nisbet (Cambridge: Cambridge University Press, 1991), 86.

28. Ibid., 87.

29. Ibid., 282.

30. Ibid., 292.

31. Ibid., 298.

32. G. W. F. Hegel, *Lectures on the Philosophy of World History*, ed. H. B. Nisbet (Cambridge: Cambridge University Press, 1977), 177.

33. Ibid., 185.

34. Ibid., 190.

Chapter 5: Pope Leo XIII and His Legacy

1. See Gerald A. McCool, *Catholic Theology in the Nineteenth Century* (New York: Seabury Press, 1977), 59–67, 88–105.

2. See Leonard E. Boyle, OP, "A Remembrance of Pope Leo XIII: The Encyclical *Aeterni Patris*," in *One Hundred Years of Thomism*, ed. Victor B. Brezik, CSB (Houston: Center for Thomistic Studies, 1981), 11. The *Syllabus* should be consulted along with Pope Pius IX's December 8, 1864, encyclical letter *Quanta Cura*.

3. See Owen Chadwick, *A History of the Popes, 1830–1914* (Oxford: Clarendon Press, 1998), 168–184.

4. *Aeterni Patris*; English translation from *The Papal Encyclicals, 1878–1903*, ed. Claudia Carlen Ihm (Ann Arbor: Pierian Press, 1990), 2:17–18. All quotes from papal encyclicals are taken from this edition.

5. Ibid., 18.

6. Ibid., 20.

7. Ibid., 23.

8. Ibid.

9. Ibid.

10. Ibid., 25.

11. Ibid., 26.

12. See Brezik, *One Hundred Years of Thomism*, 16.

13. Ibid., 17.

14. It is indeed strange that a Catholic theologian or teacher would have been forbidden to teach natural law at this time. Many of the most important Catholic manuals of philosophy from this period include sections on natural law. A good example would be the *Institutiones Philosophicae* of Matteo Liberatore. Part three of this work has an extensive treatment of natural law. See Matteo Liberatore, *Institutiones Philosophicae* (Rome: Typis Civilitatis Catholicae, 1869) 3:355–384.

15. See *Catholic Theology in the Nineteenth Century*, 136.

16. Ibid., 137.

17. See Brezik, *One Hundred Years of Thomism*, 20–24.

18. See *Libertas*, in Ihm, *Papal Encyclicals*, 2:171.

19. See especially *Prima secundae*, q. 91, art. 2 and 4. In the encyclical, Leo has also taken ideas from several other sections of the *Treatise on Law*.

20. *Libertas*, 179.

21. See *Church and State Through the Centuries*, ed. Sidney Z. Ehler and John B. Morrall (London: Burns and Oates, 1954), 234–235.

22. *Libertas*, 180.

23. Ibid., 179.

24. From *Sapientiae Christianae*, in Ihm, *Papal Encyclicals*, 2:213.

25. *Rerum Novarum*, in ibid., 243.

26. Ibid., 244.

27. See Ernest L. Fortin, "Sacred and Inviolable: *Rerum Novarum* and Natural Rights," in *Human Rights, Virtue, and the Common Good* (Lanham, Md.: Rowman and Littlefield, 1996), 196–212.

28. *Rerum Novarum*, 252.

29. Ibid., 244.

Chapter 6: The Survival of Tradition

1. See John A. Gade, *The Life of Cardinal Mercier* (New York: Charles Scribner's Sons, 1935), 21.

2. Ibid., 54.

3. Ibid., 81

4. See Louis de Raeymaeker, "La actitud del cardenal Mercier en materia de investigación filosófica," *Sapientia* 6 (1951): 254–259.

5. Gade, *Life of Cardinal Mercier*, 174.

6. Ibid., 78–90.

7. *Cardinal Mercier: Pastorals, Letters, Allocutions, 1914–1917*, ed. Joseph F. Stillemans (New York: P. J. Kenedy and Sons, 1917), 114–115.

8. Ibid., 237.

9. See John Dunaway, *Jacques Maritain* (Boston: Twayne, 1978), 16–17.

10. The powerful influence of Leon Bloy on Jacques and Raïssa Maritain is well established. Bloy, in fact, was the godfather of both. See "In Homage to Our Dear Godfather Leon Bloy," in Jacques Maritain, *Untrammeled Approaches*, ed. and trans. Bernard Doering (Notre Dame, Ind.: University of Notre Dame Press, 1997), 27–45.

11. For a brief but accurate assessment of Maritain as a Thomist, see Gerald A. McCool, SJ, *From Unity to Pluralism: The Internal Evolution of Thomism* (New York: Fordham University Press, 1989), 114–117.

12. Yves R. Simon, "Jacques Maritain: The Growth of a Christian Philosopher," in *Jacques Maritain: The Man and His Achievement*, ed. Joseph W. Evans (New York: Sheed and Ward, 1963), 7.

13. Bernard E. Doering, *Jacques Maritain and the French Catholic Intellectuals* (Notre Dame, Ind.: University of Notre Dame Press, 1983), 107–125.

14. Ibid., 105.

15. Ibid., 116–117.

16. Jacques Maritain, *Man and the State* (Chicago: University of Chicago Press, 1951), 176–177.

17. Ibid., 183.

18. Ibid., 183–184.

19. Ibid., 84–85.

20. Ibid., 84.

21. Ibid., 94.

22. *Pacem in Terris*, in *The Papal Encyclicals, 1958–1981*, ed. Claudia Carlen Ihm (Ann Arbor: Pierian Press, 1990), 5:108.

23. Ibid. 108.

24. Ibid., 111.

25. Thomism has clearly declined since the Second Vatican Council, but some scholars may have exaggerated the extent of this decline. Gerald A. McCool has remarked, "The history of the modern Neo-Thomist movement, whose *magna charta* was *Aeterni Patris*, reached its end at the Second Vatican Council," in *From Unity to Pluralism*, 230. I disagree with McCool on this issue. Many Thomists are still quite active in America, Canada, Europe, and Latin America. For a more balanced view, see Brian J. Shanley, OP, *The Thomist Tradition* (Dordrecht: Kluwer Academic, 2002), 1–20.

It is also a fact that Pope John Paul II was a strong defender of Thomistic principles.

26. *Veritatis Splendor,* English trans. in *Origins* 23, no. 18 (October 14, 1993): 310.

27. Indeed, for Thomas the first precept of natural law is that good is to be pursued and done, and evil is to be avoided. The best explanation of this principle is found in *Summa Theologicae,* 1, 2, q. 94, art. 2.

28. *Veritatis Splendor,* 312.

29. Ibid., 313.

30. Here I must take issue with Ernest L. Fortin, who has argued that John Paul tries to downplay the thought of Thomas Aquinas in this encyclical. See "From *Rerum Novarum* to *Centesimus Annus:* Continuity or Discontinuity?" in *Human Rights, Virtue, and the Common Good* (Lanham, Md.: Rowman and Littlefield, 1996), 227–229. My reading suggests the exact opposite. In fact, I would argue that John Paul II is perhaps the strongest defender of Thomistic principles among the Roman pontiffs of the twentieth century.

31. *Centesimus Annus,* in *Origins* 21, no. 1 (May 16, 1991). This passage appears in section 17, 8.

32. Ibid.

33. *Fides et Ratio,* in *Origins* 28, no. 19 (October 22, 1998). This passage appears in section 5, 320.

34. Ibid.

35. Ibid, section 90, 341.

36. Michael Bertram Crowe, *The Changing Profile of the Natural Law* (The Hague: Martinus Nijhoff, 1977), 288.

37. John Finnis, *Aquinas: Moral, Political, and Legal Theory* (Oxford: Oxford University Press, 1998).

38. Ibid., 137–138.

39. Ibid., 118.

40. Alasdair MacIntyre, *Whose Justice? Which Rationality?* (Notre Dame, Ind.: University of Notre Dame Press, 1988), 198.

41. Finnis, *Aquinas,* 152.

42. Ibid., 152–153.

43. Ibid., 307.

44. Ibid., 314–315.

45. Germain G. Grisez, "The First Principle of Practical Reason: A Commentary on the *Summa Theologiae,* 1–2, Question 94, Article 2," *Natural Law Forum* 10 (1965): 168–201.

46. Ibid., 184.

47. "Bonum et ens sunt idem secundum rem, sed differunt secundum rationem tantum. Quod sic patet. Ratio enim boni in hoc consistit quod aliquid sit appetibile, unde Philosophus in I *Ethic.* dicit quod bonum est quod omnia appetunt. Manifestum est autem quod unumquodque est appetibile

secundum quod est perfectum, nam omnia appetunt suam perfectionem. Intantum est autem perfectum unumquodque inquantum est actu. Unde manifestum est quod instantum est aliquid bonum inquantum est ens, esse enim est actualitas omnis rei, ut ex superioribus patet." *Summa Theologiae*, 1, q. 5, art. 1. The English translation is that of the Fathers of the English Dominican Province, revised by Daniel J. Sullivan.

48. For an excellent discussion of this notion, see Eleonore Stump and Norman Kretzmann, "Being and Goodness," in *Being and Goodness: The Concept of the Good in Metaphysics and Philosophical Theology*, ed. Scott Mac-Donald (Ithaca, N.Y.: Cornell University Press, 1991), 98–128.

49. Grisez, "First Principle," 187.

50. Ibid., 200.

51. "In rebus evidenter apparet quod *esse appetunt naturaliter*: unde et si qua corrumpi possunt, naturaliter corrumpentibus resistunt, et tendunt illuc ubi conserventur, sicut ignis sursum et erra deorsum. Secundum hoc autem esse habent omnia quod Deo assimilantur, qui est ipsum esse subsistens: cum omnia sint solum quasi esse participantia. Omnia igitur appetunt quasi ultimum finem Deo assimilari.

"Praeterea. Res omnes creatae sunt quaedam imagines primi agentis, scilicet Dei: *agens* enim *agit sibi simile*. Perfectio autem imaginis est ut repraesentet suum exemplar per similitudinem ad ipsum: ad hoc enim imago constituitur. Sunt igitur res omnes propter divinam similitudinem consequendam sicut propter ultimum finem." *Summa Contra Gentiles* 3.19, ed. Ceslai Pera OP, Petro Marc, OSB, and Petro Caramello (Rome: Marietti, 1961) 3:22. English translation from St. Thomas Aquinas, *Summa Contra Gentiles, Book Three: Province*, part 1, trans. Vernon J. Bourke (Notre Dame, Ind.: University of Notre Dame Press, 1975), 76.

52. On the question of non-ontological natural law, Lloyd L. Weinreb has noted, "Natural law's contemporary proponents . . . have accepted the burden of providing an unmetaphysical grounding for their position." *Natural Law and Justice* (Cambridge, Mass.: Harvard University Press, 1987), 101. Although this observation does not apply to all of the modern defenders of natural law, it certainly does hold true for the doctrine defended by Finnis and Grisez.

Bibliography

Acosta, José de. *De Procuranda Indorum Salute.* Ed. V. Abril, C. Baciero, J. Barrientos, A. García, F. Maseda, L. Pereña, and D. Ramos. Madrid: Consejo Superior de Investigaciones Científicas, 1984.

Andrés Martín, Melquíades. *La teología española en el siglo XVI.* 2 vols. Madrid: Biblioteca de Autores Cristianos, 1977.

Aquinas, St. Thomas. *Commentary on Aristotle's Nicomachean Ethics.* Trans. C. I. Litzinger, OP. Notre Dame, Ind.: Dumb Ox Books, 1993.

———. *In Decem Libros Ethicorum Aristotelis ad Nicomachum Expositio.* Ed. Raymundi M. Spiazzi, OP. Rome: Marietti, 1964.

———. *Liber de Veritate Catholicae Fidei contra Errores Infidelium seu Summa Contra Gentiles.* Ed. Petro Caramello, Petro Marc, OSB, and Ceslai Pera, OP. 3 vols. Rome: Marietti, 1961.

———. *Summa Contra Gentiles.* Trans. Vernon J. Bourke. 4 vols. Notre Dame, Ind.: University of Notre Dame Press, 1975.

———. *Summa Theologiae.* 60 vols. New York and London: Blackfriars, 1963–1975.

———. *The Treatise on Law.* Ed. Robert J. Henle, SJ. Notre Dame, Ind.: University of Notre Dame Press, 1993.

Aristotle. *The Complete Works of Aristotle.* Ed. Jonathan Barnes. 2 vols. Princeton, N.J.: Princeton University Press, 1984.

Báñez, Domingo. *The Primacy of Existence in Thomas Aquinas.* Trans. Benjamin S. Llamzon. Chicago: Regnery, 1966.

———. *Scholastica Commentaria in Primam Partem Summae Theologicae S. Thomae Aquinatis.* Ed. Luis Urgano, OP. Madrid: Editorial FEDA, 1934.

Bethell, Leslie, ed. *The Cambridge History of Latin America.* 11 vols. Cambridge: Cambridge University Press, 1984.

Billy, Dennis J., and Terence Kennedy, eds. *Some Philosophical Issues in Moral Matters: The Collected Ethical Writings of Joseph Owens.* Rome: Editiones Academiae Alphonsianae, 1996.

Blumenthal, H. J., and R. A. Markus, eds. *Neoplatonism and Early Christian Thought.* London: Variorum Publications, 1981.

Bowlin, John. *Contingency and Fortune in Aquinas's Ethics*. Cambridge: Cambridge University Press, 1999.

Braybrooke, David. *Natural Law Modernized*. Toronto: University of Toronto Press, 2001.

Brett, Annabel S. *Liberty, Right and Nature: Individual Rights in Later Scholastic Thought*. Cambridge: Cambridge University Press, 1997.

Breuer, Isaac. *Concepts of Judaism*. Ed. Jacob S. Levinger. Jerusalem: Israel Universities Press, 1974.

Brezik, Victor B., CSB, ed. *One Hundred Years of Thomism*. Houston: Center for Thomistic Studies, 1981.

Cavalier, Robert J., James Gouinlock, and James P. Sterba, eds. *Ethics in the History of Western Philosophy*. New York: St. Martin's Press, 1989.

Chadwick, Owen. *A History of the Popes, 1830–1914*. Oxford: Clarendon Press, 1998.

Cicero, Marcus Tullius. *De Legibus*. Ed. and trans. Clinton Walker Keyes. Cambridge, Mass.: Harvard University Press, 1977.

Copenhaver, Brian P., and Charles B. Schmitt. *Renaissance Philosophy*. Oxford: Oxford University Press, 1992.

Copleston, Frederick, SJ. *A History of Philosophy*. Vol. 3, *Late Medieval and Renaissance Philosophy*. New York: Image Books, 1963.

Crowe, Michael Bertram. *The Changing Profile of the Natural Law*. The Hague: Martinus Nijhoff, 1977.

Darwall, Stephen. *Philosophical Ethics*. Boulder, Colo.: Westview Press, 1998.

Davies, Brian. *The Thought of Thomas Aquinas*. Oxford: Clarendon Press, 1992.

De Raeymaeker, Louis. "La actitud del cardenal Mercier en materia de investigación filosófica." *Sapientia* 6 (1951): 250–261.

———. *The Philosophy of Being*. Trans. Edmund H. Ziegelmeyer. St. Louis, Mo.: B. Herder, 1954.

Di Blasi, Fulvio. *God and the Natural Law: A Rereading of Thomas Aquinas*. South Bend, Ind.: St. Augustine Press, 2006.

Dietze, Gottfried. *Liberalism Proper and Proper Liberalism*. Baltimore: Johns Hopkins University Press, 1985.

DiJoseph, John. *Jacques Maritain and the Moral Foundation of Democracy*. Lanham, Md.: Rowman and Littlefield, 1996.

Doering, Bernard E. *Jacques Maritain and the French Catholic Intellectuals*. Notre Dame, Ind.: University of Notre Dame Press, 1983.

Doyle, John P. "Francisco Suárez: On Preaching the Gospel to People Like the American Indians." *Fordham International Law Journal* 15, no. 4 (1991–1992): 879–951.

———. "Suárez On the Reality of the Possibles." *The Modern Schoolman* 45 (1967): 29–48.

Dunaway, John M. *Jacques Maritain*. Boston: Twayne, 1978.

Dupré, Louis. *Passage to Modernity.* New Haven: Yale University Press, 1993.

Ehler, Sidney Z., and John B. Morrall, eds. *Church and State Through the Centuries.* London: Burns and Oates, 1954.

Elders, Leo J., SVD. *The Metaphysics of Being of St. Thomas Aquinas in a Historical Perspective.* Trans. John Dudley. Leiden: E. J. Brill, 1993.

Elliott, John H. *Spain and Its World, 1500–1700.* New Haven: Yale University Press, 1989.

Evans, Joseph W. *Jacques Maritain: The Man and His Achievement.* New York: Sheed and Ward, 1963.

Ferrater Mora, José. "Suárez and Modern Philosophy." *Journal of the History of Ideas* 14 (1953): 528–547.

Fichter, Joseph H. *Man of Spain: Francis Suárez.* New York: Macmillan, 1940.

Finnis, John. *Aquinas: Moral, Political, and Legal Theory.* Oxford: Oxford University Press, 1998.

———. "Aquinas on *ius* and Hart on Rights: A Response to Tierney." *Review of Politics* 64 (Summer 2002): 407–410.

———. *Natural Law and Natural Rights.* Oxford: Clarendon Press, 1982.

Fortin, Ernest L. *The Birth of Philosophic Christianity.* Lanham, Md.: Rowman and Littlefield, 1996.

———. *Classical Christianity and the Political Order: Reflections on the Theologico-Political Problem.* Lanham, Md.: Rowman and Littlefield, 1996.

———. *Human Rights, Virtue, and the Common Good: Untimely Meditations on Religion and Politics.* Lanham, Md.: Rowman and Littlefield, 1996.

Gade, John A. *The Life of Cardinal Mercier.* New York: Charles Scribner's Sons, 1935.

Gallagher, David M., ed. *Thomas Aquinas and His Legacy.* Washington, D.C.: Catholic University of America Press, 1994.

George, Robert P. *Natural Law, Liberalism, and Morality.* Oxford: Clarendon Press, 1996.

Gibson, Charles. *Spain in America.* New York: Harper and Row, 1966.

Gilson, Etienne. *Being and Some Philosophers.* 2nd ed. Toronto: Pontifical Institute of Medieval Studies, 1952.

Gordley, James. *The Philosophical Origins of Modern Contract Doctrine.* Oxford: Clarendon Press, 1991.

Goyette, John, et al. *St. Thomas Aquinas and the Natural Law Tradition: Contemporary Philosophical and Theological Perspectives.* Washington, D.C.: Catholic University of America Press, 2004.

Gracia, Jorge J. E. *Suárez On Individuation, Metaphysical Disputation V: Individual Unity and Its Principle.* Milwaukee: Marquette University Press, 1982.

Green, Otis H. "A Note on Spanish Humanism: Sepúlveda and His Translation of Aristotle's *Politics.*" *Hispanic Review* 8 (1940): 339–342.

Grisez, Germain G. "The First Principle of Practical Reason: A Commentary on the *Summa theologiae*, 1–2, Question 94, Article 2." *Natural Law Forum* 10 (1965): 168–201.

Grotius, Hugo. *The Law of War and Peace*. Trans. Francis W. Kelsey. New York: Bobbs-Merrill, 1925.

Guyer, Paul. *The Cambridge Companion to Kant*. Cambridge: Cambridge University Press, 1992.

Hales, E. E. Y. *The Catholic Church in the Modern World*. Garden City, N.Y.: Hanover House, 1958.

Hanke, Lewis. *Aristotle and the American Indians*. Chicago: Regnery, 1959.

Hegel, G. W. F. *Lectures on the Philosophy of World History*. Ed. H. B. Nisbet. Cambridge: Cambridge University Press, 1975.

Hibbs, Thomas, and John O'Callaghan, eds. *Recovering Nature: Essays in Natural Philosophy, Ethics, and Metaphysics in Honor of Ralph McInerny*. Notre Dame, Ind.: University of Notre Dame Press, 1999.

Hittinger, Russell. *A Critique of the New Natural Law Theory*. Notre Dame, Ind.: University of Notre Dame Press, 1987.

Hume, David. *An Enquiry Concerning the Principles of Morals*. Ed. Tom L. Beauchamp. Oxford: Oxford University Press, 1998.

Ihm, Claudia Carlen, ed. *The Papal Encyclicals, 1740–1981*. 5 vols. Ann Arbor: Pierian Press, 1990.

Jaffa, Harry V. *Thomism and Aristotelianism*. Westport, Conn.: Greenwood Press, 1979.

John Paul II. "*Centesimus Annus*." *Origins* 21, no. 1 (May 16, 1991): 1–24.

———. "*Fides et Ratio*." *Origins* 28, no. 19 (October 22, 1998): 317–347.

———. "*Veritatis Splendor*." *Origins* 23, no. 18 (October 14, 1993): 297–334.

Kainz, Howard P. *Natural Law: An Introduction and Re-examination*. Chicago: Open Court, 2004.

Kazcor, Christopher. *Proportionalism and the Natural Law Tradition*. Washington, D.C.: Catholic University of America Press, 2002.

Kenny, Anthony. *A New History of Western Philosophy*. 3 vols. Oxford: Clarendon Press, 2004–2006.

Kent, Peter C., and John F. Pollard. *Papal Diplomacy in the Modern Age*. Westport, Conn.: Praeger, 1994.

Kessler, Eckhard, Jill Kraye, Charles B. Schmitt, and Quentin Skinner, eds. *The Cambridge History of Renaissance Philosophy*. Cambridge: Cambridge University Press, 1988.

Klocker, Harry R., SJ. *Thomism and Modern Thought*. New York: Appleton-Century-Crofts, 1962.

Knight, David M., SJ. "Suárez's Approach to Substantial Form." *The Modern Schoolman* 39 (1962): 219–239.

Knowles, David. *The Evolution of Medieval Thought*. London: Longmans, 1962.

Kraynak, Robert P. *Christian Faith and Modern Democracy*. Notre Dame, Ind.: University of Notre Dame Press, 2001.

Kretzmann, Norman. *The Metaphysics of Creation: Aquinas's Natural Theology in Summa contra gentiles II*. Oxford: Clarendon Press, 1999.

Kretzmann, Norman, Anthony Kenny, Jan Pinborg, and Eleonore Stump. *The Cambridge History of Later Medieval Philosophy*. Cambridge: Cambridge University Press, 1982.

Kretzmann, Norman, and Eleonore Stump, eds. *The Cambridge Companion to Aquinas*. Cambridge: Cambridge University Press, 1993.

Las Casas, Bartolomé de. *In Defense of the Indians*. Ed. and trans. Stafford Poole, CM. DeKalb: Northern Illinois University Press, 1992.

———. *Obras Completas*. Vol. 2, *De Unico Vocationis Modo*. Ed. Paulino Castañeda and Antonio García del Moral, OP. Madrid: Alianza Editorial, 1990.

———. *The Only Way*. Ed. Helen Rand Parish, trans. Francis Patrick Sullivan, SJ. New York: Paulist Press, 1992.

Liberatore, Matthaei. *Institutiones Philosophicae*. 3 vols. Rome: Typis Civilitatis Catholicae, 1869.

Lisska, Anthony J. *Aquinas's Theory of Natural Law*. Oxford: Oxford University Press, 1996.

———. "Bentham and Recent Work in Natural Law: Towards Reconstructing An Unstilted Theory." *Current Legal Problems 1998*, ed. M. D. A. Freeman, 51. Oxford: Oxford University Press, 1998.

Locke, John. *Essays on the Law of Nature*. Ed. W. von Leyden. Oxford: Oxford University Press, 1988.

Lohr, Charles H. *Latin Aristotle Commentaries: II Renaissance Authors*. Florence: Leo S. Olschki Editore, 1988.

Losada, Angel. *Juan Ginés de Sepúlveda a través de su "Epistolario" y nuevos documentos*. Madrid: Consejo Superior de Investigaciones Científicas, 1973.

———, ed. *Apología de Juan Ginés de Sepúlveda contra Fray Bartolomé de Las Casas y de Fray Bartolomé de Las Casas contra Juan Ginés de Sepúlveda*. Madrid: Editora Nacional, 1975.

MacDonald, Scott, ed. *Being and Goodness: The Concept of the Good in Metaphysics and Philosophical Theology*. Ithaca, N.Y.: Cornell University Press, 1991.

MacDonald, Scott, and Eleonore Stump, eds. *Aquinas's Moral Theory: Essays in Honor of Norman Kretzmann*. Ithaca, N.Y.: Cornell University Press, 1999.

MacIntyre, Alasdair. *After Virtue: A Study in Moral Theory*. Notre Dame, Ind.: University of Notre Dame Press, 1981.

———. *The Tasks of Philosophy: Selected Essays*. Cambridge: Cambridge University Press, 2006.

————. *Whose Justice? Which Rationality?* Notre Dame, Ind.: University of Notre Dame Press, 1988.

Maritain, Jacques. *Man and the State*. Chicago: University of Chicago Press, 1951.

————. *Untrammeled Approaches*. Trans. Bernard Doering. Notre Dame, Ind.: University of Notre Dame Press, 1997.

McCool, Gerald A. *Catholic Theology in the Nineteenth Century*. New York: Seabury Press, 1977.

————. *From Unity to Pluralism*. New York: Fordham University Press, 1989.

————. *The Neo-Thomists*. Milwaukee: Marquette University Press, 1994.

McGrade, Arthur Stephen. *The Political Thought of William of Ockham: Personal and Institutional Principles*. Cambridge: Cambridge University Press, 1974.

McInerny, Ralph. *Aquinas on Human Action*. Washington, D.C.: Catholic University of America Press, 1992.

————. *Boethius and Aquinas*. Washington, D.C.: Catholic University of America Press, 1990.

————. *Ethica Thomistica: The Moral Philosophy of Thomas Aquinas*. Washington, D.C.: Catholic University of America Press, 1982.

Meron, Theodor. *Human Rights Law-Making in the United Nations: A Critique of Instruments and Process*. Oxford: Clarendon Press, 1986.

————. *Praeambula Fidei: Thomism and the God of the Philosophers*. Washington, D.C.: Catholic University of America Press, 2006.

Miller, Fred D. *Nature, Justice, and Rights in Aristotle's Politics*. Oxford: Oxford University Press, 1995.

Monahan, Arthur P. *From Personal Duties Towards Personal Rights: Late Medieval and Early Modern Political Thought, 1300–1600*. Toronto: McGill-Queens University Press, 1994.

Ockham, William. *Philosophical Writings*. Ed. Philotheus Boehner. London: Nelson, 1962.

Owens, Joseph. *The Doctrine of Being in the Aristotelian Metaphysics*. Toronto: Pontifical Institute of Mediaeval Studies, 1978.

————. "The Number of Terms in the Suarezian Discussion of Essence and Being." *The Modern Schoolman* 34 (1957): 147–191.

————. *Towards a Christian Philosophy*. Washington, D.C.: Catholic University of America Press, 1990.

Pagden, Anthony. *The Fall of Natural Man: The American Indian and the Origins of Comparative Ethnology*. Cambridge: Cambridge University Press, 1982.

Patterson, Annabel. *Early Modern Liberalism*. Cambridge: Cambridge University Press, 1997.

Peccorini, Francisco. "Knowledge of the Singular: Aquinas, Suárez, and Recent Interpreters." *The Thomist* 38 (1974): 606–655.

Pereña, Vicente Luciano, ed. *Misión de España en América*. Madrid: Consejo Superior de Investigaciones Científicas, 1956.

Redmond, Walter Bernard. *Bibliography of the Philosophy in the Iberian Colonies of America*. The Hague: Nijhoff, 1972.

Rhonheimer, Martin. *Natural Law and Practical Reason*. Trans. Gerald Malsbary. New York: Fordham University Press, 2000.

Rommen, Heinrich A. *The Natural Law: A Study in Legal and Social History and Philosophy*. Indianapolis: Liberty Fund, 1998.

Schall, James V. *Jacques Maritain: The Philosopher in Society*. Lanham, Md.: Rowman and Littlefield, 1998.

Scheler, Max. *Formalism in Ethics and Non-Formal Ethics of Value: A New Attempt Toward the Foundation of an Ethical Personalism*. Trans. Manfred S. Frings and Robert L. Funk. Evanston, Ill.: Northwestern University Press, 1973.

Schneewind, Jerome B. *The Invention of Autonomy: A History of Modern Moral Philosophy*. Cambridge: Cambridge University Press, 1998.

Schockenhoff, Eberhard. *Natural Law and Human Dignity: Universal Ethics in an Historical World*. Trans. Brian McNeil. Washington, D.C.: Catholic University of America Press, 2003.

Sepúlveda, Juan Ginés de. *Demócrates Segundo o de las justas causas de la guerra contra los indios*. Ed. and trans. Angel Losada. Madrid: Consejo Superior de Investigaciones Científicas, 1984.

Shanley, Brian J. *The Thomist Tradition*. Dordrecht: Kluwer Academic, 2002.

———, ed. *One Hundred Years of Philosophy*. Washington, D.C.: Catholic University of America Press, 2001.

Sigmund, Paul E. "The Catholic Tradition and Modern Democracy." *The Review of Politics* 49 (Fall 1987): 530–548.

Skinner, Quentin. *The Foundations of Modern Political Thought*. Cambridge: Cambridge University Press, 1978.

Soto, Domingo de. *De la justicia y del derecho*. Ed. Marcelino González, OP, and Venancio Diego Carro, OP. 4 vols. Madrid: Instituto de Estudios Políticos, 1968.

Stanlis, Peter J. *Edmund Burke and the Natural Law*. Ann Arbor: University of Michigan Press, 1958.

Strauss, Leo. *Natural Right and History*. Chicago: University of Chicago Press, 1971.

———. *What Is Political Philosophy?* Chicago: University of Chicago Press, 1988.

Suárez, Francisco. *Disputaciones Metafísicas*. Ed. and trans. Sergio Rábade Romeo, Salvador Caballero Sánchez, and Antonio Puigcerver Zanón. 7 vols. Madrid: Editorial Gredos, 1960–1966.

———. *Selections from Three Works of Francisco Suárez, S.J.* Ed. James Brown Scott. 2 vols. Oxford: Clarendon Press, 1944.

Sumner, L. W. *The Moral Foundation of Rights.* Oxford: Clarendon Press, 1987.

Theron, Stephen. *Natural Law Reconsidered: The Ethics of Human Liberation.* New York: Peter Lang, 2002.

Tierney, Brian. *The Idea of Natural Rights.* Atlanta: Scholars Press, 1997.

———. "Natural Law and Natural Rights: Old Problems and Recent Approaches." *The Review of Politics* 64 (Summer 2002): 389–406.

Torrell, Jean-Pierre. *Saint Thomas Aquinas: The Person and His Work.* Trans. Robert Royal. Washington, D.C.: Catholic University of America Press, 1996.

Tuck, Richard. *Natural Rights Theories.* Cambridge: Cambridge University Press, 1979.

Veatch, Henry B. *For an Ontology of Morals: A Critique of Contemporary Ethical Theory.* Evanston, Ill.: Northwestern University Press, 1971.

———. *Human Rights: Fact or Fancy?* Baton Rouge: Louisiana State University Press, 1985.

———. *Swimming Against the Current in Contemporary Philosophy: Occasional Essays and Papers.* Washington, D.C.: Catholic University of America Press, 1990.

Vitoria, Francisco de. *Political Writings.* Ed. Anthony Pagden and Jeremy Lawrance. Cambridge: Cambridge University Press, 1991.

Weinberg, Julius R. *A Short History of Medieval Philosophy.* Princeton, N.J.: Princeton University Press, 1964.

Weinreb, Lloyd L. *Natural Law and Justice.* Cambridge, Mass.: Harvard University Press, 1987.

Weisheipl, James A. *Friar Thomas D'Aquino: His Life, Thought, and Works.* Washington, D.C.: Catholic University of America Press, 1983.

Wells, Norman J. "Capreolus on Essence and Existence." *The Modern Schoolman* 38 (1960): 1–24.

Westberg, Daniel. *Right Practical Reason: Aristotle, Action, and Prudence in Aquinas.* Oxford: Clarendon Press, 1994.

White, Kevin. *Hispanic Philosophy in the Age of Discovery.* Washington, D.C.: Catholic University of America Press, 1997.

Wilkerson, T. E. *Natural Kinds.* Aldershot, UK: Avebury, 1995.

Williams, Bernard. *Ethics and the Limits of Philosophy.* Cambridge, Mass.: Harvard University Press, 1985.

Wippel, John F. *The Metaphysical Thought of Thomas Aquinas.* Washington, D.C.: Catholic University of America Press, 2000.

Zavala, Silvio. *La filosofía política en la Conquista de América.* México: Fondo de Cultura Económica, 1984.

Zigliara, Thoma Maria. *Summa Philosophica.* 3 vols. Paris: Gabriel Beauchesne, 1909.

Index

abolition, ix–x
Adorno, Theodor, 2
Aeterni Patris, xv–xvi, 65, 70, 77, 105;
 Thomism, 69
Africans, 62–64
Albert the Great, 3
American Constitution, 83
anthropology, 94
Aristotelian tradition, 31
Aristotle: Aquinas, 14–15, 38, 42–43;
 being, xiii; children, 18, 64;
 happiness, 64; Hegel, 64; Hobbes,
 28; human dignity, 38; morality,
 xiii; natural law, xiii, 21–22;
 natural servitude, 35–36, 37–38,
 39; Sepúlveda, 31; Soto, 25;
 Vitoria, 37–38
Augustine (Saint), 9

Báñez, Domingo, xiv–xv, 7–8; Catejan,
 39; New World, 39; Spanish Con-
 quest, 39; Vitoria, 39
being, 10; Aristotle, xiii; Kant, 55;
 moral action, 15; morality, 14, 93,
 96; perfection of, 15; rights, 96.
 See also ens
Bellarmine, Robert, 115; James I, 52
Bernanos, George, 81–82
Bloy, Leon, 81–82, 119
Boethius, 11, 105
Brett, Annabel, 25–26
Breuer, Isaac, 116
Buzzetti, Vincenzo, 69

Cano, Melchior, xiv–xv, 7; New World,
 42; Suárez, 42; Vitoria, 42
capital punishment, 17; Kant, 57
Capreolus, John, 6
Catejan (Cardinal), 6–7, 105; Báñez, 39;
 Soto, 40; Suárez, 40; Vitoria, 40
Catholic Emancipation Act in 1829, 53
Centessimus Annus, 94
charity, 68
Charles V (Emperor), 32
children: Aquinas, 18; Aristotle, 18, 64;
 deformities in, 19; Finnis, 96; hap-
 piness, 18; Hegel, 64; Kant, 56; Leo
 XIII, 74–75; value of, 18
Christian philosophy: faith, 66–67
Civilta Cattolica, 70
Claudel, Paul, 81–82
common good, 57; human rights, 28;
 natural rights, 86–87
Comte, Auguste, 2
"concept," 59–60
Cortest, Tomas Daniel, v
Costa, José de, 38–39
creation, 109
"Critical School," 2
Crowe, Michael, 94
Cursus Conimbricenisium, 7

d'Azeglio, Luigi Taparelli, 69–70
De hebdomadibus, 11
De Iure Belli, 27
De iustitia et iure, 24, 34
De Legibus, ac Deo Legislatore, 26–27